James Martin
Easy Every Day

James Martin
Easy Every Day

MITCHELL BEAZLEY

contents

meat

Loins of Lamb with Cumin and Almond-dressed Artichokes

Jerusalem artichokes are one of the winter vegetables I greatly enjoy using in cooking, despite their knobbly skins. The name, incidentally, has nothing to do with the Holy City, but is derived from the Italian word for sunflower – *girasole* – to which the plant is related. In this recipe, I pan-fry them in butter and oil, and use a fruity redcurrant balsamic vinegar from California, sweet almond oil and cumin for flavouring. Loins of lamb (also known as cannons) are the long, narrow, round pieces of meat found in the saddle of a lamb.

SERVES 4

4 whole loin lamb fillets, about 200g (7oz) each

4 tbsp whole cumin seeds

600g (1lb 5oz) Jerusalem artichokes, peeled (use a swivel peeler)

60g (2¼oz) butter

2 tbsp olive oil

6 tbsp redcurrant balsamic vinegar (or good-quality, aged balsamic vinegar)

½ small red pepper, deseeded and finely chopped

2 tbsp chopped fresh chervil or parsley

2 tbsp almond oil

sea salt and freshly ground black pepper

Trim the loins of all fat so that they are neatly round in shape. Lightly crush the cumin seeds using a pestle and mortar, or use an electric grinder but take care not to grind them too finely. Reserve 1 tbsp of the cumin seeds for later use.

Sprinkle the ground cumin on a sheet of foil or paper and roll the loins in the spice to coat. Set aside.

Slice the artichokes thinly (drop them immediately into lemony water if preparing ahead to prevent discoloration, since they quickly turn brown once cut). Heat about three-quarters of the butter with 1 tbsp of the olive oil in a frying pan. Add the sliced artichokes and pan-fry for about 10 minutes, stirring occasionally, until tender. Add seasoning, then stir in the vinegar, the reserved cumin seeds, the red pepper, half the chervil or parsley and the almond oil. Simmer for about a further 5 minutes. Keep warm.

Meanwhile, preheat the oven to 200°C/400°F/gas mark 6. Heat the remaining olive oil and butter in a heavy-based frying pan, add the loins and cook until evenly browned all over. Transfer to a roasting pan and cook in the oven for about 12 minutes until slightly springy when pressed with the back of a fork. This indicates that they are medium rare. If you like well-done lamb, cook for a few minutes longer. Let the lamb stand for 5 minutes, then slice into medallions.

Spoon the artichokes on to the centre of warmed serving plates. Arrange the lamb on top and sprinkle over the remaining chervil or parsley. Trickle over any pan juices and serve.

Variation If you can't buy artichokes, you could substitute baby parsnips.

A simple, full-flavoured, no-nonsense way of cooking a nice leg (or rolled shoulder) of lamb. It's really an adaptation of a recipe I cooked frequently at Anthony Worrall Thompson's 190 Queen's Gate restaurant in South Kensington, London, where we would braise lamb shanks for 24 hours until they were meltingly tender. Boy, were they popular! We would get through hundreds of shanks each week. These days, you have to pay a premium price for them.

Anchovy and Garlic-studded Roast Lamb

SERVES 4

1 boned and rolled leg or shoulder of lamb, about 2.5–3kg (5½lb–6½lb)

50g can anchovies in oil, drained

7–8 fat garlic cloves, peeled and halved lengthways

about 15 sprigs fresh rosemary

olive oil (optional)

sea salt and freshly ground black pepper

Preheat the oven to 180°C/350°F/gas mark 4.

Stab the lamb about 15 times or so with a sharp-pointed knife.

Pat the drained anchovies dry with kitchen paper and cut in half widthways. Roll each piece of anchovy around a halved garlic clove and a rosemary sprig, then push into the stab holes. You may need to make more holes.

If the lamb is very lean on top, brush over a little oil to moisten. Season the lamb, place in a roasting pan and roast in the oven for 1–1¼ hours until the meat is very tender. When the lamb is cooked, let it rest for about 15 minutes before carving.

Serving note Serve the lamb in thickly carved slices with Celeriac Remoulade (*see* page 146).

Pork and Tarragon Rillettes

Rillettes are classically made with pork, but can be made from rabbit, duck and chicken as well. The meat used here is cooked pork, such as left-over roast meat. Many people are put off by the use of fat in the preparation of rillettes, but this recipe uses less than usual, and brings the meat and fat together only at the last moment (the traditional recipe cooks the meat in the fat). You must serve the pâté on hot toast or bread as this allows the fat to melt into the bread, making it all much easier to eat and much more digestible. With this dish you may need to use more salt than usual as this will bring out the flavour of the pork.

SERVES 2

225g (8oz) cooked pork meat

55g (2oz) pork lard or dripping

4 sprigs fresh tarragon, chopped

3 tbsp chopped fresh parsley

sea salt and freshly ground black pepper

Cut the pork into dice. Melt the fat on the stove.

Place the pork in a blender, together with the tarragon, parsley, and some salt and pepper. While mixing, pour the melted fat into the blender. Try to do this quickly, as the pork should not be a purée, but still quite chunky.

Remove from the blender and serve with thick chunks of hot toasted bread.

Potato, Truffle and Parma Ham Terrine

Despite the luxurious nature of this starter, it doesn't take long to put together. However, you need to assemble the terrine the night before so that it can be pressed overnight in the refrigerator. Buy the Parma ham freshly sliced and laid out neatly on waxed paper, to prevent the slices from sticking together. Truffle slices are available packed in oil – you can use some of the oil for the dressing.

SERVES 6

650g (1lb 7oz) firm potatoes, preferably maris piper or desirée

about 12 slices Parma ham

150g (5½oz) butter, melted

50g (1¾oz) sliced black truffles (optional but memorable)

2 tbsp chopped fresh chives

sea salt and freshly ground black pepper

DRESSING

1 tbsp finely chopped black truffle (optional)

2 plum tomatoes, deseeded and finely chopped

3 tbsp balsamic vinegar

juice and grated zest of 1 lemon

100ml (3½fl oz) olive oil

1 tbsp chopped fresh parsley

Boil the potatoes in their skins in a saucepan of lightly salted water for about 15 minutes until tender. Drain and leave to cool a little. Peel while still lukewarm, then cut into 1cm (½in) slices.

Line a 450g (1lb) terrine mould or loaf tin with clingfilm, pressing it into the sides firmly and smoothly. Line the mould or tin with half the slices of Parma ham, allowing the ends of the slices to hang over the sides.

Arrange a layer of sliced potatoes in the base of the mould or tin, then spoon over about one third of the melted butter, add some truffle slices (if using), and cover with Parma ham. Sprinkle with chives and seasoning. Add another layer of potatoes, spoon over more melted butter, then add more truffle slices (if using) and another layer of ham. Sprinkle with chives and seasoning. Add the remaining potatoes, butter and truffle slices, then finish with a layer of ham. Fold over the hanging pieces of ham. Cover the whole terrine with clingfilm and press down lightly to firm.

Place a flat plate on top of the terrine and weigh down with a large can or something similar. Chill in the refrigerator overnight.

Before serving, mix together all the ingredients for the dressing. Demould the terrine by shaking out on to a board. Peel off the clingfilm and cut into 6 even slices. Place each slice on a serving plate and spoon around the dressing. Serve lightly chilled.

Pork and beans are natural partners. They can be chic and sophisticated or homely and satisfying. This is an adaptation of a dish I make using a trio of pork cuts – lean loin, fillet and a good chunk of fattier belly. But you can use just one of these cuts, or opt for a rolled shoulder of pork that combines lean and fat in one joint. The apple and potato mash (see Serving note) with the balsamic-flavoured butter beans make this a truly memorable dish.

Roast Pork with Balsamic Butter Bean Broth

SERVES 6

2 tbsp Dijon mustard

2 tbsp clear honey

1 pork joint (loin, rolled lean belly or boneless rolled shoulder), about 1.3kg (3lb), rinded

500ml (18fl oz) fresh chicken stock

2 tbsp balsamic vinegar

400g can butter beans, drained and rinsed

a good knob of butter

2 tbsp coarse-grain mustard, e.g. Pommery or Gordons (optional)

2–3 tbsp chopped mixed fresh herbs, e.g. parsley, dill, oregano and basil

sea salt and freshly ground black pepper

Preheat the oven to 180°C/350°F/gas mark 4.

Spread the Dijon mustard and then the honey over the pork and season well. Roast the joint in the oven for about 1¾ hours until tender.

Meanwhile, place the stock and vinegar in a saucepan, bring to the boil and continue boiling until reduced by half. Add the beans and cook for about 5 minutes. Season, stir in the butter and set aside.

When the pork is cooked, spread the top with the coarse-grain mustard (if using) and press on the chopped fresh herbs. Let the joint stand for 10 minutes to firm up a little before carving into neat slices. Meanwhile, reheat the beans and serve with the sliced pork.

Serving note Serve this dish with a simple but effective apple and potato mash – grated apple beaten into standard mashed potato. For best results use good mashing potatoes, e.g. maris piper, king edward or desirée, and golden delicious or granny smith apples.

Grilled Pork with a Spicy Borlotti Bean, Pancetta and Cabbage Stew

Good roast pork with crunchy crackling is one of the joys of eating. When I was about eight, I used to nick the crackling from under the grill while father was watching television, and eat it with some rock salt at the back door (for a quick exit). Pork is very reasonably priced and this is a great way to use it for a heavy, filling dish.

SERVES 4

225g (8oz) pancetta, diced

½ red onion, peeled and finely chopped

4 garlic cloves, peeled and finely chopped

½ small carrot, finely chopped

4 pork chops, about 200g (7oz) each

1 x 400g can borlotti beans, drained and rinsed

500ml (18fl oz) fresh chicken stock

1 fresh green chilli, deseeded and finely diced

8 fresh savoy cabbage leaves

20g (¾oz) fresh flat-leaf parsley, chopped

sea salt and freshly ground black pepper

First sauté the pancetta in a pan without any oil (there is enough fat in it already). Once the pancetta is crisp, add the onion, garlic and carrot to the pan and cook for about a minute.

Season the pork chops well and place under a preheated hot grill for about 12 minutes altogether, turning them over every few minutes. When the pork is cooked, the fat should be a nice brown colour.

While the pork is cooking, add the beans, chicken stock and chilli to the onion mix and bring to the boil. Cook for about 5 minutes.

Thinly slice the cabbage leaves, add to the stew, and cook for about a further 2 minutes.

Remove the chops from the grill and finish the stew with lots of chopped parsley. Spoon the stew on to four plates, place the chops on the top and serve.

Caramelized Braised Beef

We have become so used to eating quick-cooked beef in the form of steaks or stir-fries that we are in danger of forgetting just how delicious it can be if cooked long and slow until it can be pulled apart in tender shreds. This is an easy-to-prepare dish, cooked pot-roast style. Buy the best piece of roasting beef you can afford, such as rolled sirloin, but having said that, a top rump or silverside joint will give lots of flavour if cooked for a further 30 minutes–1 hour.

SERVES 4

1 tbsp olive oil

1 sirloin beef joint (but see recipe introduction), preferably traditionally or organically reared, about 1kg (2lb 4oz)

2 carrots, chopped

3 shallots, peeled and chopped

1 leek, sliced

1 tbsp caster sugar

2 fat garlic cloves, peeled and crushed

300ml (½ pint) fresh chicken stock

300ml (½ pint) red wine

5 tbsp balsamic vinegar

50g (1¾oz) butter

sea salt and freshly ground black pepper

Preheat the oven to 180°C/350°F/gas mark 4.

Heat the oil in a frying pan, add the beef joint and brown all over.

Remove the beef joint and add the vegetables, shaking the pan and stirring the vegetables to give them just a little colour.

Add the sugar, garlic, stock, wine, vinegar and butter to the vegetables. Bring to the boil, then transfer the vegetables and juices into a small roasting pan. Sit the beef joint on top, season well and cover loosely with a sheet of foil. Don't tuck the foil around the sides, but just shape it roughly around the outside of the joint.

Braise in the oven for about 1½ hours, uncovering twice during the cooking time, if possible, and spooning the pan juices over the beef.

Remove the meat and leave to stand for 10 minutes before carving. Serve with the caramelized vegetables and pan juices spooned over.

Serving note I like to serve this dish with a creamy risotto, topped with shavings of Parmesan. You may prefer to serve it with mash.

This is food for one, but can easily be expanded to feed more, if you've got enough beef left over. The pesto is very easy to make and just involves puréeing the ingredients. I love this with a baked potato (done in a microwave) with lots of butter. It would be quite tasty in a sandwich as well.

Cold Beef with Parsley Pesto and Red Onion

SERVES 1

55g (2oz) fresh parsley

2 canned anchovy fillets

1 garlic clove, peeled

about 6–8 tbsp extra-virgin olive oil

4 slices cold cooked beef

1 red onion, peeled and thinly sliced

sea salt and freshly ground black pepper

Purée the parsley, anchovy fillets and garlic in a food processor, then add enough oil to make a mayonnaise-type consistency.

Season the pesto with salt and pepper, and serve it with the beef and red onion.

Beef Steaks with Sun-blushed Tomatoes and Parsley

Pomodorello tomatoes are lightly sun-dried Italian tomatoes in olive oil (I call them 'sun-blushed') and they are wonderfully sweet and succulent. Serve them snipped into salads, with pasta or on pizzas or bruschetta. Alternatively, just enjoy nibbling them on their own. As this recipe reveals, I also like to use them for jazzing up pan-fried steaks.

SERVES 2

2 beef steaks (fillet, sirloin or rump), about 200g (7oz) each

a good knob of butter

1 tbsp olive oil

125g (4½oz) pomodorello tomatoes

1 tbsp chopped fresh parsley

1 tbsp chopped fresh basil

1 tbsp balsamic vinegar

sea salt and freshly ground black pepper

Heat a non-stick frying pan and, when you feel a good heat rising, add the steaks to the dry pan. Cook for a minute or so before adding the butter and oil. This helps to colour the steaks well.

After cooking for 1 minute, turn the steaks over and cook the other side. Timing depends on the thickness of the steaks and how you like them. Allow about 5 minutes in total for medium-rare steaks. They should feel slightly springy when pressed with the back of a fork. Season well during cooking, then remove to warmed dinner plates.

Meanwhile, chop the tomatoes and place in a bowl with half the chopped herbs, the vinegar and seasoning. Add the tomato mixture to the pan and heat through for 1–2 minutes. Spoon on top of the steaks and sprinkle over the remaining herbs. Grind over black pepper and serve pronto!

The fact that black pudding is made from pigs' blood mixed with oatmeal, suet and onion may not appeal to you, but I consider it one of the true essentials in breakfast cooking. The best come from good butchers' shops, as they are usually made fresh on the premises. These have much more flavour and taste than the commercial branded black puddings. I believe black puddings should be sliced and pan-fried. The cooking time is important as well as the heat of the pan, and you don't need much fat. A cooked slice of black pudding should be slightly crisp on the edges but moist in the centre.

Black Pudding with Caramelized Apple and Cider

SERVES 2

1 golden delicious apple

55g (2oz) butter

1 tbsp caster sugar

175g (6oz) black pudding, cut into 1cm (½in) slices

50ml (2fl oz) cider

sea salt and freshly ground black pepper

Place two hot pans on the stove and heat to a high heat while you prepare the apple. Core the apple whole, then cut it in half and slice each half into five slices.

Divide the butter between the two pans, and put the sugar in one of them. Place the black pudding into the non-sugared pan, reduce the heat and cook for 2–3 minutes, turning occasionally.

When the sugar and butter in the other pan have started to turn golden brown, add the apple slices. Turn up the heat and quickly caramelize the apple: about 3 minutes. Pour in the cider to deglaze the pan, stirring well, and season quickly with salt and pepper.

To serve, either put the apple mixture and the black pudding into separate bowls or plates for the two of you to help yourselves from, or arrange the apple on the two plates with the black pudding on top.

You can cook this dish in just five minutes flat using a good-quality, ready-made fresh pasta or a decent dried variety, tossed with some fresh or dried sage.

Calves' Liver with Port-flavoured Pan Juices

SERVES 2

25g (1oz) butter

1 tbsp olive oil

250g (9oz) calves' liver, thinly sliced and cut in half lengthways

about 4 tbsp port or Madeira

2 tsp red wine vinegar

100ml (3½fl oz) fresh beef or chicken stock

250g (9oz) fresh or 200g (7oz) dried ribbon pasta

½ tbsp chopped fresh sage or a good pinch of dried sage

1 tbsp crème fraîche (optional)

sea salt and freshly ground black pepper

Heat a large saucepan of lightly salted water until boiling for the pasta.

Meanwhile, heat half the butter with the oil in a frying pan until hot and no longer foaming. Add the liver and fry for 1–2 minutes on each side until well browned and just firm when pressed with the back of a fork. Season in the pan, then remove to a warmed plate and keep warm.

Add the port or Madeira to the pan, bring to the boil and allow to bubble until reduced by half. Add the vinegar and cook for a few seconds. Pour in the stock and bring to the boil, stirring. Continue to boil until reduced by half.

Meanwhile, add the pasta to the pan of boiling water and cook for 2–3 minutes for fresh pasta or according to the packet instructions for dried pasta until just tender. Drain, then toss with the remaining butter and the fresh or dried sage.

Season the pasta well and divide between two warmed serving plates. Lay the liver over the top (you may want to slice this into attractive pieces). Whisk the crème fraîche (if using) into the sauce in the pan, check the seasoning and spoon over the liver. Serve immediately.

Seared Calves' Liver with Balsamic Vinegar and Onions

Like most people, I love onions, and feel this traditional dish needs lots of them. I've also brought the dish up to date slightly by adding balsamic vinegar to the onions. Balsamic vinegar, like wine, is available at different ages and the older it is, the mellower, smoother and more expensive it is. Commercial balsamic vinegars found in supermarkets are made more speedily, and therefore will be sharper in flavour, not so pure, and considerably cheaper. However, it's fine to use the cheaper balsamics in this recipe.

SERVES 2

3 large white onions, peeled and sliced

55g (2oz) butter

375ml (13fl oz) red wine

250ml (9fl oz) fresh beef stock

1 tbsp olive oil

2 slices calves' liver (avoid wafer-thin slices), about 175g (6oz) each

4 tbsp balsamic vinegar

sea salt and freshly ground black pepper

Place the onions in a pan with half the butter and all the red wine and beef stock, and cook until the liquid has reduced by about four-fifths. This can take up to 30 or 40 minutes.

When the onions are nearly ready, heat a frying pan until it is very hot. Melt the remaining butter in it with the olive oil (to stop the butter burning) and cook the liver quickly, getting colour on both sides but remembering to keep it pink in the middle. This will take no longer than about 2 minutes.

Add the vinegar to the onions and season well.

Serve the liver on the plate with the onions on the top. I like to put another piece of butter on the onions.

chicken
& duck

Use legs or breasts for this dish. Using breasts would be quicker, if more expensive, but I think they both taste the same when you get your teeth into them. Free-range chickens are worth buying, as are corn-fed. The yellow colour does actually come from the corn the birds have eaten; they are not dyed as some people think.

Chicken with Plum and Sun-dried Tomatoes

SERVES 2

2 chicken legs (or breasts), about 225g (8oz) each

1 tbsp olive oil

2 tbsp clear honey

½ small red onion, peeled and sliced

2 garlic cloves, peeled and sliced

6 plum tomatoes, quartered

100g (3½oz) sun-dried tomatoes in oil

15g (½oz) fresh basil

sea salt and freshly ground black pepper

Preheat the oven to 200°C/400°F/gas mark 6.

In a hot pan, sear the chicken in the olive oil to colour both sides well. Remove from the pan, drizzle with honey and bake in the oven until cooked (about 10 minutes for breasts, 25 minutes for legs).

Meanwhile, place the onion and garlic in a pan. Add the fresh tomatoes, and the sun-dried plus their oil. Bring to the boil and remove from the heat straight away. Season with salt and pepper, and leave to cool a little. Then add some ripped leaves of fresh basil.

To serve, just put the tomato mixture on plates with the chicken on top.

Cheat's Coq au Vin

One evening I invited a new girlfriend to supper, intending to wow her with the classic French dish, coq au vin. Typically, I was late back from work. Undaunted and unabashed, I picked up a bargain bucket of fried chicken from the local takeaway and spent the 15 minutes before she arrived stripping the chicken of its crispy coating and making a simple red wine sauce. The meal was a great success, so either she didn't notice or was just too polite to say anything!

SERVES 4

8 cooked joints of chicken, on the bone – a mixture of breasts and thighs or legs

25g (1oz) butter

1 tbsp olive oil

4 garlic cloves, peeled and chopped

2 red onions, peeled and sliced

150g (5½oz) pancetta, in one piece, rinded and chopped

250g (9oz) button mushrooms

a good pinch of dried thyme

300ml (½ pint) red wine

500ml (18 floz) fresh chicken stock

150ml (¼ pint) double cream

2 tbsp chopped fresh parsley

sea salt and freshly ground black pepper

Skin the cooked chicken pieces and set aside.

Heat the butter with the oil in a large cast-iron or flameproof casserole, add the garlic, onions and pancetta and sauté for about 5 minutes until softened. Add the mushrooms and thyme and sauté for 5 minutes.

Pour in the wine, bring to the boil and continue boiling, uncovered, for about 5 minutes until the sauce is reduced by half. Pour in the stock and bring back to the boil.

Season and add the chicken to the sauce. Reduce the heat and simmer for a good 5 minutes until the chicken is thoroughly heated through. Remove the chicken pieces to a warmed serving dish with a slotted spoon.

Increase the heat and boil the sauce until reduced by about half. Reduce the heat, stir in the cream and gently heat through.

Pour the sauce over the chicken pieces, sprinkle with parsley and serve.

Serving note Creamy mash or rice goes particularly well with this dish.

Paillard of Chicken with Mozzarella, Prosciutto and Sage

The combination of chicken, mozzarella, plum and sage here is really successful, and the whole lot is like one big, tall, messy pizza. Trendy chefs are even using thin slices of salmon as a base for different pizza-style toppings – whatever next?

SERVES 4

4 boneless chicken breasts, about 225g (8oz) each

4 tbsp olive oil, plus extra for drizzling

12 sage leaves

8 tbsp plum chutney (*see* page 288)

2 balls of buffalo mozzarella cheese, about 150g (5½oz) each

8 slices prosciutto

8 sprigs fresh basil

sea salt and freshly ground black pepper

Cut the chicken breasts in half, but not all the way through – just enough to open the breasts out flat (called butterflying). Season the chicken well, and cook in a hot sauté pan in the olive oil, colouring both sides well: about 8–10 minutes altogether.

When the chicken is cooked, place 3 sage leaves along with 2 tbsp plum chutney on the top of each breast.

Remove the mozzarella from the packets and drain. Chop into dice. Divide the cheese into 4 piles, and place a pile on each butterflied chicken. Finish with the slices of prosciutto. Drizzle with olive oil and season well.

Place under a preheated hot grill to crisp the bacon. It should take only a few minutes. This will also melt the cheese.

Place the chicken on plates and pour the juices remaining in the pan over the top. Garnish with the fresh basil.

The 'crunch' here is created by the polenta topping on the chicken. The rocket pesto gives another kick to an already spicy dish, but it's great to get the heart pumping. I was nineteen when I first took a girl out, and this was the dish I cooked for her on our first date. It took me two hours to do the shopping; one and a half to do the cooking; I spent £50 on food, wine and flowers; and two hours and £200 on new clothes. All that hassle, and it turned out she was vegetarian. She ended up with meat-free pot noodles – and I ate it all.

Crunchy Chilli Chicken with Rocket Pesto

SERVES 2

2 chicken breasts, about 225g (8oz) each

1 tbsp olive oil

sea salt and freshly ground black pepper

TOPPING

2 plum tomatoes

¼ red chilli, deseeded

2 canned anchovy fillets

¼ red pepper, deseeded

¼ small red onion, peeled

½ garlic clove, peeled

2 tbsp olive oil

115g (4oz) instant polenta

ROCKET PESTO

115g (4oz) rocket leaves

½ garlic clove, peeled

1 tbsp pine nuts, toasted

8 tbsp olive oil

To make the topping, place the tomatoes, chilli, anchovy, red pepper, onion and garlic into a blender and purée to a rough paste. Add the olive oil and season very well with salt and pepper. Combine this purée with the instant polenta in a bowl.

Clean the blender and place all the pesto ingredients in it. Blend to a fine purée. Remove from the blender and leave to one side.

Preheat the oven to 200°C/400°F/gas mark 6.

Season the chicken breasts with salt and pepper and seal in a hot pan with the olive oil for a few minutes on each side, to colour the flesh. Place the breasts on an oven tray and top each with a thick coating of the polenta mixture.

Bake in the oven for about 20 minutes, to cook the chicken through and allow the topping to go crunchy. If the chicken is cooked before the topping is crisp, remove from the oven and place under a preheated grill.

Place the breasts on plates, and serve with a green salad and a dollop of the rocket pesto on the side.

Pan-fried Chicken with Chilli Beans, Fennel and Pancetta

This is a great meal for the end of a hard-working day. Buy the ingredients on your way home from work and within half an hour you'll have a great-tasting dish full of punchy flavours. All it needs is a loaf of crusty bread and a simple green salad – oh, and a glass or two of crisp white wine.

SERVES 4

2 tbsp extra virgin olive oil, plus extra for drizzling

4 skinless, boneless chicken breasts, about 150g (5½oz) each

2 shallots, peeled and chopped

4 garlic cloves, peeled and chopped

1 large red chilli, deseeded and chopped

1 small bulb of fennel, thinly sliced

1 x 400g can flageolet beans, drained and rinsed

juice and grated zest of 1 lemon

3 tbsp chopped mixed fresh herbs, e.g. parsley, mint or basil

8 thin slices pancetta

sea salt and freshly ground black pepper

Heat a large, heavy-based, non-stick frying pan until you feel a good heat rising. Add about 1 tbsp of the oil, then add the chicken breasts and pan-fry for about 5 minutes on each side until firm when pressed with the back of a fork. Season well and set aside in the pan. They will keep warm without extra heating.

Heat the remaining oil in a separate pan, add the shallots, garlic, chilli and fennel and stir-fry for about 5 minutes until softened.

Add the beans and seasoning to taste, then heat through until piping hot. Stir in the lemon zest and juice and fresh herbs.

Meanwhile, preheat the grill until hot. Grill the pancetta until crisp, then drain on kitchen paper.

Divide the bean and fennel mixture between four warmed serving plates. Slice the chicken breasts into medallions and arrange on top, then add 2 slices of pancetta to each plate, which you can either crumble or leave whole. Drizzle over any chicken pan juices and a little extra oil.

Surf 'n' Turf, or Ranch 'n' Reef, is what the Americans call this combination of fish and meat on the same plate. I've taken the idea and further combined it with one of my favourite quick American sauces, Rockefeller, usually served with oysters. Its predominant flavours are Pernod, herbs and fennel. Once made, it is a great stuffing or you could fold it into some pasta. The tomato chips, which are also good as finger food, are similar to sundried tomatoes in that both have a strong intense flavour once the juices have been dried out. Make them well in advance.

Rockefeller Chicken with Lobster and Tomato Chips

SERVES 2

2 boneless chicken breasts (with skin on), about 225g (8oz) each

3 tbsp olive oil

1 cooked lobster, about 450g (1lb)

1 x 200g can plum tomatoes

1 x 190g jar pesto (or homemade, *see* page 110)

3 tbsp chopped fresh parsley

2 tbsp chopped celery

2 tbsp chopped shallot

4 tbsp chopped watercress

1 garlic clove, peeled and chopped

3 tbsp chopped fennel

3 tbsp fresh white breadcrumbs

125ml (4fl oz) Pernod

2 tbsp chopped fresh chives

2 tbsp chopped fresh basil

2 tbsp chopped fresh flat-leaf parsley

½ cucumber

sprigs of fresh herbs

sea salt and freshly ground black pepper

TOMATO CHIPS
225g (8oz) plum tomatoes

The day before you want to serve the chicken, make the tomato chips. Slice the tomatoes and arrange on greaseproof paper on a baking tray. Put into the oven at the very lowest heat possible (110°C/225°F/gas mark ¼, or less if possible) and leave overnight or until the tomato slices have become crisp. Cool and store in an airtight container.

Season the chicken breasts well with salt and pepper, then place into a frying pan with about 1 tbsp of the olive oil and cook.

Remove the shell from the lobster body and claws. Keep the lobster tail shell (cut in half lengthways) and the two antennae off the head for garnish. Discard the remainder of the head and shells. Keep the tail and claw flesh to one side.

Purée the canned tomatoes and pour the pesto and the tomato purée into two small squeezy bottles.

Put the parsley, celery, shallot, watercress, garlic, fennel and half the breadcrumbs with another 1 tbsp of the oil into a hot wok and cook for a second or two. Add 75ml (2½fl oz) of the Pernod and flame. Season quickly. Add the remaining breadcrumbs and the chopped herbs and leave to one side.

Cut the cucumber in half and remove the seeds. Slice lengthways on a mandoline to produce wide strips. Warm these through in one pan with 1 tbsp of the Rockefeller sauce and 1 tbsp of the pesto, and warm the lobster flesh and tail shell pieces through in another pan with the remaining oil. Pour the remaining Pernod over the lobster and flame.

Arrange the cucumber strips on the plates as a base. Cut the cooked chicken breasts into three slices each, and place on top, with the lobster flesh, and the lobster tail shell and antennae. Carefully squeeze the pesto and tomato purée on to the plates in a decorative pattern. Finish with 1 tbsp of the Rockefeller sauce on the top. Garnish with the tomato chips and sprigs of fresh herbs.

Left-over Chicken with a Mint, Chickpea and Lemon Salad

A superb salad made with canned chickpeas, chicken and rocket. I made this salad (without the chicken) on *Celebrity Ready Steady Cook* with Gaby Roslin (who is a vegetarian). I've specified chicken breast, but any cooked chicken can be used, or you could even buy cooked chicken from a supermarket. You could also purée the salad ingredients as an interesting vegetarian hummus-type dip.

SERVES 2

1 x 250g can chickpeas, drained and rinsed

2 tbsp chopped fresh mint

juice and grated zest of 1 lemon

1 tbsp olive oil

100g (3½oz) rocket leaves

2 cooked chicken breasts, about 225g (8oz) each

sea salt and freshly ground black pepper

Place the chickpeas in a bowl with the chopped mint, lemon juice and zest and olive oil. Season with salt and pepper.

Spoon the chickpeas on to a plate, leaving the dressing behind. Put the rocket leaves on the top and pour over the chickpea dressing.

Put the chicken on the top and serve. (If you have time, some diced cucumber and garlic mixed with yoghurt is a good garnish.)

Devils on Horseback

I love to take traditional recipes and give them a twist. Here I've put chicken livers inside prunes, instead of the usual stuffing of almonds. Chicken livers are cheap, very tasty and easy to cook in dishes such as this, or in pâtés or stuffings. Cook them to pink only, as overcooked liver is as tough as old boots. They are also great in stews and casseroles for added flavour.

MAKES 12

6 chicken livers

55g (2oz) butter

cayenne pepper

12 stoned, ready-to-eat prunes

6 rashers of good smoked streaky bacon, cut in half

sea salt and freshly ground black pepper

To prepare the livers, trim away any excess stringy sinew, and any yellow-coloured parts. Cut the livers in half. Wash and pat dry.

In a hot pan, sauté the livers quickly in the butter for about 1 minute until just sealed, seasoning them with salt and pepper. Remove from the pan and dust with cayenne pepper; as much or as little as you like.

Stuff each prune with a half liver, then wrap up in the bacon strips and secure with wooden cocktail sticks.

Place under a preheated grill until the bacon is crisp, about 1–2 minutes on each side. If you allow the 'devils' to cool slightly, you can remove the cocktail sticks without them falling apart.

Roast Marinated Duck Breast with a Chicory Tarte Tatin

This is about as fussy as I get with food, but what a superb dish. The commonest breeds of duck are the Aylesbury and the Barbary; the Aylesbury has a lighter-coloured flesh and is fattier. Buy duck breasts with their skin on, as it is here that most of the flavour is concentrated. Be sure almost to blacken the skin on the breasts (as described below) before putting them in the oven as this creates a nice crisp skin on the top and a lovely nutty flavour.

SERVES 2

2 duck breasts (with skin on), about 200g (7oz) each

sea salt and freshly ground black pepper

MARINADE

½ carrot, grated

1 garlic clove, peeled and chopped

½ red onion, peeled and diced

55g (2oz) clear honey

50ml (2fl oz) white wine

3 tbsp chopped fresh coriander

2 tbsp chopped fresh mint

juice and grated zest of 1 orange

4 tbsp dark soy sauce

4 tbsp sesame seeds

CHICORY TARTE TATIN

4 heads chicory

250ml (9fl oz) orange juice

200ml (7fl oz) white wine

3 tbsp chopped fresh coriander

1 garlic clove, peeled and finely chopped

55g (2oz) caster sugar

100g (3½oz) pre-rolled puff pastry

SAUCE

100ml (3½fl oz) white wine

115g (4oz) butter, softened

Put all the ingredients for the marinade in a china or earthenware bowl. Place the duck in it and leave for at least 2 hours; overnight is best.

Preheat the oven to 200°C/400°F/gas mark 6.

Cut the chicory in half lengthways. Place in an ovenproof dish and pour on the orange juice and wine. Add the chopped coriander and garlic and season with salt and pepper, then cover with foil and place in the oven for about 20 minutes. Remove from the oven and take the chicory out of the juice, but keep the juice for later.

In a clean, non-stick, ovenproof pan, about 20cm (8in) in diameter, melt the sugar to a golden-brown caramel and place the drained chicory on top of this. Cut the pre-rolled puff pastry into a circle about 1cm (½in) bigger than the pan. Place the pastry on the top and tuck in the edges down the side of the pan to seal in the chicory. Place the pan in the oven and bake at the same temperature as above for 15 minutes, until the pastry is cooked.

Meanwhile, drain the duck, then place in a very hot, dry pan. Seal on both sides, making sure the skin side is blackened slightly. Place the duck on an oven tray and roast in the oven at the same temperature as above for about 10 minutes, keeping it pink in the middle (or about 12–13 minutes if you want it well done).

To make the sauce, put the juice from the chicory into a pan with the white wine and reduce until there's hardly any liquid remaining. Turn the heat down and add the soft butter, bit by bit with a whisk, until you have a thickened sauce. Season and leave to one side.

Remove the duck and tarte tatin from the oven. Turn the tart out while hot on to a large serving plate, inverting it so that the pastry is the base and the chicory is at the top. Slice the duck thinly over the top, spoon the sauce around and serve.

This is a quick and impressive dinner-party dish. You'll need to track down a spicy fennel and pine nut pâté called *pâté di finocchietto* from a good deli. All the other ingredients are readily available. For the duck breasts, use either Lincolnshire duck or the darker French Barbary breasts which are larger. Serve with pasta or creamy mash.

Duck Breasts with Fennel Pâté and Apples

SERVES 2

1 bulb of fennel, thinly sliced, fronds reserved for garnishing

1 golden delicious apple, cored and cut into 8 wedges

1 fat garlic clove, peeled and crushed

1 shallot, chopped

2 tbsp olive oil

a knob of butter

1 tbsp clear honey

2 duck breasts, about 150–200g (5½–7oz) each

90g pâté di finocchietto

2 tbsp toasted pinenuts

sea salt and freshly ground black pepper

Place the fennel, apple, garlic and shallot in a saucepan with the oil and butter. Heat until it starts to sizzle, then sauté gently for about 10 minutes, stirring carefully until softened. Turn up the heat towards the end of the cooking time to colour the apple wedges. Season and keep warm.

Heat the honey in a non-stick frying pan. Slash the fat side of the duck breasts 3–4 times, add to the pan and fry, skin side down, for about 5 minutes until the skin becomes a glossy dark brown. Be careful not to let the fat begin to smoke. If it does, pour it away.

Turn the breasts and cook on the other side for 5 minutes. The breasts are nicest served slightly pink inside, which you can check by pressing them with the back of a fork. They should feel lightly springy but not too bouncy. If you prefer them less pink, cook for a few minutes longer, but don't overcook. Season the duck in the pan, then remove and leave to stand for 5 minutes.

Slice the breasts diagonally into medallions. Spoon the fennel and apple mixture on to the centre of warmed serving plates. Arrange the duck pieces on top. Beat the pâté until runny, then trickle over the duck. Scatter over the pine nuts and garnish with the reserved fennel fronds. (In a restaurant, I would deep-fry the fennel fronds, but you may well think this is not worth the effort.)

Honeyed Duck Confit with Crispy Seaweed and Creamy Mash

You can buy, or prepare yourself, plump, tender duck legs that have been cooked deliciously slowly in their own fat. Known as duck confit, they are ideal for many dishes.

SERVES 2

2 duck legs, confited in their own fat, homemade or from a can or jar

4 tbsp clear honey

3 tbsp olive oil

leaves stripped from 2–3 sprigs fresh thyme

300g (10½oz) mashing potatoes, eg maris piper, king edward or desirée, chopped

3 tbsp hot milk

a small knob of butter

100ml (3½fl oz) red wine

250ml (9fl oz) fresh chicken stock

55g (2oz) crispy seaweed

sea salt and freshly ground black pepper

Preheat the oven to 180°C/350°F/gas mark 4.

Scrape the fat from the duck legs and place them in a roasting pan. (Don't waste the fat – it's wonderful for frying eggs or roasting potatoes.)

Whisk the honey and oil together and smear over the duck legs. Sprinkle over the thyme leaves. Roast the legs in the oven for about 20 minutes, spooning the honey glaze over them 2–3 times.

Meanwhile, boil the potatoes in a saucepan of lightly salted water for about 15 minutes until just tender. Drain, then mash with a fork, gradually beating in the hot milk, butter and plenty of seasoning.

Place the wine and stock in a saucepan, bring to the boil and continue boiling until reduced by two-thirds. Season well.

Spoon the mashed potato on to the centre of warmed serving plates, sprinkle the seaweed round the mash and sit the duck legs on top. Scrape any meaty bits from the roasting pan and sprinkle over, then pour over the reduced red wine sauce and serve immediately.

Ingredients note To make your own duck confit, take two duck legs and weigh them. Measure 15g (½oz) salt per 1kg (2lb 4oz) meat and sprinkle the salt with fresh thyme over the duck legs. Store in the fridge for at least 12 hours. Melt duck fat (available in cans from delis) in a pan over a low heat and bring to a simmer. Place the chilled duck legs in the fat and cook very gently for 1½–2 hours; do not boil. Take off the heat and leave to cool in the fat.

fish

Puy lentils, small and grey-green in colour, are grown in France. With a very distinctive flavour, they keep their shape and colour when cooked. They are available canned as well, which here speeds the whole thing up considerably. Although any type of lentil will do for this recipe, *lentilles de Puy* really are the best. These flavoured lentils go really well with seared scallops and chicken as well as with the cod here.

Cod with Cumin and Coriander Lentils

SERVES 2

½ carrot, finely diced

¼ leek, finely diced

¼ red onion, peeled and finely diced

25g (1oz) butter

150ml (5fl oz) red wine

1 x 400g can Puy lentils, drained and rinsed

2 thick pieces cod (with skin on), about 225g (8oz) each

½ tsp balsamic vinegar

1 tsp ground cumin

15g (½oz) fresh coriander, roughly chopped

sea salt and freshly ground black pepper

Sauté the carrot, leek and onion in a pan in half the butter until softened. Then add the red wine and drained lentils. Warm through gently while you cook the cod.

In a non-stick frying pan, place the cod, skin side down, in the remaining butter and sauté for about 2–3 minutes. Turn over, and cook for a further 2 minutes. Try to avoid turning it more than once, as cod will fall to bits very easily if it is fresh.

Season the lentils with the vinegar, ground cumin, salt and pepper, then fold in the chopped fresh coriander.

Serve the lentils with the cod on the top, and a glass of white wine.

Tip Buy the best quality, freshest cod. It should be pure white in colour, and it shouldn't smell of anything, not even of fish. To hold the fish together, as its flesh is very flaky, get it cut at least 2.5cm (1in) thick, and keep the skin on. The skin also crisps up in the cooking and adds considerably to the flavour.

This is new British food with a twist. We are all great cod lovers in this country, but sadly, as stocks dwindle, so do the size and quality of the fish on sale. We love thick, meaty middle-cut fillets of cod, but more often than not we now get thinner pieces from younger fish. They still taste great, but just be prepared to pay a high price for them. Coastal regions of the UK still keep the tradition of selling small pots of tasty little pinky-brown shrimps set in a little butter, known as potted shrimps. To make them even more 'shrimpy', I like to add a few chopped cold-water prawns. Sometimes sold as North Atlantic prawns, these have a full, sweet-salty taste of the wild ocean. Seafood from icy-cold waters tastes much nicer than its tropical-water cousins.

Pan-fried Cod with Vanilla Shrimp Butter

SERVES 4

2 small tubs potted shrimps, about 50g (1¾oz) each, at room temperature

100g (3½oz) unsalted butter, softened

100g (3½oz) peeled cold-water cooked prawns, thawed if frozen and patted dry

2 tbsp chopped fresh parsley

1 vanilla pod

3 tbsp extra virgin olive oil

4 cod fillets, about 150–200g (5½–7oz) each

1 tbsp balsamic vinegar

100g (3½oz) mixed salad leaves

sea salt and freshly ground black pepper

Mix the potted shrimps with the unsalted butter in a bowl. Chop the prawns quite finely and add to the shrimp mixture with the parsley and plenty of pepper. Mix well.

Slit the vanilla pod lengthways and scrape out the seeds with the tip of a knife. Add the seeds to the shrimp butter. (Re-use the pod for making vanilla sugar – *see* Ingredients note, page 274.) Shape the shrimp butter into a log on a sheet of clingfilm and roll neatly until smooth on the outside. Chill in the refrigerator for about 30 minutes until firm.

When ready to serve, heat 1 tbsp of the oil in a large frying pan. Season the cod and fry, skin side down, on a medium heat for about 5–7 minutes until the flesh is about three-quarters cooked (you can check this simply by pressing the flesh: it should feel just a little springy). Turn the fish over carefully to cook the other side, but turn off the heat so that it cooks gently.

Cut the butter into neat discs, allowing about 2 per serving. Add any end pieces of butter to the pan to flavour the cod.

Mix the remaining oil with the vinegar and seasoning. Place the salad leaves in a bowl, add the dressing and toss well.

Divide the salad between serving plates. Arrange the cod fillets on the dressed leaves, with the discs of shrimp butter on top. Grind over some black pepper and serve immediately.

Cod, garlic and mashed potato are, in my opinion, the three best ingredients in the world. This dish is my favourite, being classic no-nonsense food. There's a very famous restaurant in Paris that has a speciality of fish with vanilla. Although normally associated with desserts, vanilla marries well with cod because it has the ability to bring together the other ingredients. Smoked garlic is now available in supermarkets, but normal garlic will do. And you can, of course, leave the vanilla out of the mash, as long as you add lots of milk, cream and butter.

Roast Cod with Smoked Garlic and Vanilla Mash

SERVES 4

1 vanilla pod

4 thick pieces cod fillet (with skin on but no bone), about 200g (7oz) each

4 tbsp olive oil, plus extra for drizzling

4 bulbs smoked garlic

2 sprigs fresh thyme

juice and grated zest of 1 lemon

sea salt and freshly ground black pepper

MASHED POTATO

3 estima baking potatoes

150ml (5fl oz) milk

100ml (3½fl oz) double cream

40g (1½oz) butter

Peel the potatoes, cut into large dice and place in a pan of lightly salted water. Bring to the boil and simmer for about 15 minutes until soft, then drain and leave to one side.

Split the vanilla pod and scrape out the seeds. Keep both separate.

Preheat the oven to 220°C/425°F/gas mark 7.

Season the cod well with salt and pepper, and sauté in a hot pan, skin side down, in the olive oil. When the skin is crisp – after a few minutes only – remove the pan from the heat and place the fish in an ovenproof dish, skin side up.

Break the garlic into separate cloves and remove any excess outer skin, but don't peel the cloves. Put the garlic cloves in the cod dish along with the fresh thyme and the scraped-out vanilla pod. Drizzle with olive oil and put in the oven for about 8–10 minutes.

While the cod is cooking, place the vanilla seeds in a pan with the milk and cream for the mash. Warm gently on the stove.

Place the potato in a food mixer and, with the machine beating, slowly pour on the milk and cream through a sieve. When the mash is smooth, season well and add the butter to finish.

Put some of the mash on each plate and place the cod on top, with the garlic cloves over and around. To finish, mix the lemon juice and zest into the cod juices in the pan, and pour over the lot. Serve immediately.

Brandade of Salt Cod

Brandade is a homemade salt cod pâté popular in France, but it can be found in various other guises throughout the rest of the Mediterranean. Salt cod originates from Scandinavia and was one of the mainstays of the European diet for centuries. It was also exported to the West Indies during the dark days of slavery as a high-protein food and is still popular there. You need a good-quality salt cod that is thick and still a little pliable rather than stiff and grey, from Spain or Portugal. Start preparing the dish 24 hours in advance.

SERVES 4

400g (14oz) thick-cut salt cod fillets

100ml (3½fl oz) olive oil

1 fat garlic clove, peeled and chopped

150ml (¼ pint) double cream

2 tbsp cooked mashed potato

a dribble of good-quality truffle oil (*see* Ingredients note, page 113 – optional)

juice and grated zest of 1 lemon

freshly ground black pepper

Soak the salt cod in plenty of cold water 24 hours in advance, changing the water every 6 hours or thereabouts (according to your sleep pattern!). Drain thoroughly.

Place the soaked cod in a large pan of cold water and bring to the boil. Remove from the heat and leave the cod to steep in the water as it cools. By then it will have cooked. Drain, skin and flake the fish, checking for and discarding any bones. Transfer to a food processor or blender.

Gently heat the olive oil with the garlic in a small saucepan. In a separate small saucepan, gently heat the cream until hot, then add the mashed potato with a tiny amount of truffle oil (if using). Mix well.

With the food processor or blender running, add the creamy potato, then the garlicky oil, and blend until you have a creamy, scoopable paste. Season with pepper (it won't need any salt). Add the lemon zest and juice to taste before spooning the brandade into a serving bowl.

Serving note This is great served as part of tapas with a Salad of Roasted Peppers and Olives (*see* page 173) and crusty, country-style bread.

Brill with Chinese Lardons and Green Leaves

There are some delicious Asian sauces that add instant flavour to quick marinades and pan-fries. I quickly made up this recipe on a television set with Ken Hom, the well-known Chinese chef, in my keenness to show him that a Yorkshireman could cook Chinese. The marinade has since served me well on various occasions, adding a great depth of flavour for very little effort. Brill is a meaty flat fish that is available from fishmongers. If you cannot find it, sole is a good substitute. You'll need to buy fresh pork belly rashers or a whole piece of pork belly and marinate it the night before.

SERVES 4

500g (1lb 2oz) pork belly, in one piece, or thick-cut rashers, rinded

4 brill or sole fillets, about 150g (5½oz) each

melted butter, for brushing

about 400g (14oz) pak or bok choy (Chinese greens)

1 tbsp sunflower oil

a few drops of sesame oil

sea salt and freshly ground black pepper

MARINADE

2 tbsp tomato purée

½ plump red chilli, deseeded and chopped

1 tsp Chinese five-spice powder

1 fat garlic clove, peeled and crushed

1 tbsp grated fresh root ginger or ginger purée

1 tbsp Thai fish sauce

1 tbsp dark soy sauce (preferably Tamari)

1 tbsp sake or very dry sherry

1 tbsp demerara sugar

Place the pork belly or rashers in a food bag. Blend the ingredients for the marinade in a food processor or blender to form a paste, or mix by hand, and pour into the bag. Rub well into the meat, then seal the bag, place in the refrigerator and leave to marinate overnight.

Preheat the oven to 180°C/350°F/gas mark 4.

Tip the pork and marinade into a roasting pan and cook, uncovered, for 30–40 minutes until the meat is tender and the top nicely browned. Leave to cool, then cut the meat into small cubes.

Season the brill or sole and brush with a little melted butter. Preheat the grill until hot. Grill the fish for about 5–8 minutes without turning, otherwise the flesh may break up. Set aside.

Chop the greens into big pieces. Heat the sunflower oil in a wok, add the pork cubes and stir-fry for 1–2 minutes until hot. Add the chopped greens and stir-fry quickly until wilted. Drizzle over a few drops of sesame oil to flavour and divide between warmed serving plates. Place a brill or sole fillet on top of each mound of greens and serve immediately.

This is another of my best-loved fish and sausage combinations – the majestic turbot, a meaty flat fish, and the French boudin sausage. You can use black or white boudin, which is available from many good delis. British black pudding, however, is softer and crumbles, so is not a good substitute. Soulful black-eye beans peas give this dish an American twist.

Turbot with Boudin and Black-eye Beans

SERVES 4

200g (7oz) black-eye beans, soaked overnight and drained

1 onion, peeled and chopped

2 fat garlic cloves, peeled and crushed

1 carrot, chopped

1 medium leek, chopped

2 tbsp olive oil, plus extra for brushing

250g (9oz) boudin sausage, blanc or noir, diced

450ml (16fl oz) fresh chicken stock

1 sprig fresh thyme

4 turbot, halibut or swordfish fillets, about 150g (5½oz) each, skinned

3 tbsp Forvm red wine vinegar (see Ingredients note)

a good knob of butter

2 tbsp chopped fresh parsley

2 tbsp basil oil

sea salt and freshly ground black pepper

Place the beans in a saucepan, cover with cold water and bring to the boil. Cook on a medium boil for 10 minutes. Drain and set aside. Preheat the oven to 180°C/350°F/gas mark 4.

Place the onion, garlic, carrot, leek and the olive oil in a cast-iron saucepan or flameproof casserole and heat until the contents start to sizzle. Sauté for about 5 minutes, then add the diced sausage and cook for about 3 minutes.

Add the stock and the beans. Bring to the boil and add the sprig of thyme and seasoning. Cover and transfer the pot to the oven. Cook for about 45 minutes until the beans are tender.

Brush the fish fillets with a little olive oil and season. Place in an ovenproof dish and bake, uncovered, for 10–12 minutes until the fish is just firm to the touch but not overcooked. Remove and keep warm.

Place the bean pot back on the stove, add the vinegar and cook, uncovered, for about 10 minutes until the liquid is reduced by a third. Remove the beans, vegetables and diced sausage from the broth with a slotted spoon and place on warmed serving plates.

Whisk the butter into the broth until it turns glossy, then stir in the parsley. Spoon the sauce over the beans and place the fish on the side. Drizzle around the basil oil.

Ingredients note I rate Spanish Forvm wine vinegar, used here to spike the bean broth, as possibly the best wine vinegar available. It is made from Cabernet Sauvignon wine, and is so mellow that you can almost drink it neat.

Halibut Steaks with Beansprout and Coriander Salad

Halibut is a large flat fish caught in the cold, dark waters of the North Atlantic, which gives it a fine flavour and firm texture. Sold in meaty steaks, sometimes with a small central bone, I find it suits flash pan-frying very well and teams up nicely with my Plum chutney, (see page 288), and this easy salad. This is real fusion food.

SERVES 2

200g (7oz) fresh beansprouts

2 tbsp roughly chopped fresh coriander leaves

1 shallot, peeled and finely chopped

juice and grated zest of 1 lemon

1 fat red chilli, deseeded and thinly sliced

1–2 tbsp olive oil

2 halibut steaks, about 200g (7oz) each

Plum Chutney (see page 288)

sea salt and freshly ground black pepper

Wash the beansprouts in a colander and shake dry. Tip into a bowl and add the chopped coriander, shallot, lemon zest and juice, chilli and seasoning. Mix well and set aside.

When ready to serve, heat a heavy-based frying pan until you feel a good heat rising. Add the oil, then the halibut, skin side down, and fry for 5 minutes until crispy. Carefully flip over and cook the other side for about 2 minutes until the flesh feels firm when pressed.

Divide the salad between serving plates and place a fish fillet on top. Spoon a little chutney on to each plate and serve.

In wine-growing regions of the world, food is often wrapped in vine leaves and cooked in the embers of a wood fire or barbecue, especially fish which takes just minutes to cook. You can replicate this method of cooking using greaseproof paper. Firm meaty fish, such as halibut, salmon or monkfish, are the most suitable. Capers and the aniseed-flavoured Pernod are classic accompanying flavourings.

Halibut Parcels with Capers and Pernod

SERVES 4

4 halibut steaks, about 200g (7oz) each

4 tbsp capers in brine, drained, plus extra to serve

4 tbsp Pernod

50g (1¾oz) butter, cut into 4 cubes

juice of 1 lemon

4 slices lemon

sea salt and freshly ground black pepper

Preheat the oven to 190°C/375°F/gas mark 5.

Cut four 25cm (10in) squares of greaseproof paper. Lay them flat and place a halibut steak in the centre of each. Season, then scatter each steak with 1 tbsp capers and 1 tbsp Pernod. Add a cube of butter, sprinkle over the lemon juice and top with a lemon slice.

Fold over or scrunch up the paper to form parcels and place in a baking dish. Bake the parcels in the oven for 15–20 minutes until just firm to the touch (feel through the paper).

Leave the parcels to stand for 5 minutes, then transfer each one to a warmed serving plate and spoon a few capers on the top.

Serving note Serve this dish with mashed potato, baby new potatoes or rice and a bowl of lightly cooked whole green beans.

Monkfish is a strange creature – a white fish with the smooth texture of shellfish. It slices conveniently into neat nuggets, and blends well with punchy flavours such as cracked black pepper, mustard and dill. Monkfish tails are sold ready-skinned, but ask the fishmonger to remove the long cartilaginous bone for you. Cut off as much of the grey membrane as you can before cutting into medallions – a razor-sharp filleting knife will make the task easier.

Pepper-crusted Monkfish with Mustard Dill Sauce

SERVES 4

1 monkfish tail, about 500g (1lb 2oz), filleted and skinned

about 3 tbsp whole black peppercorns, cracked with a rolling pin (*see* below)

2 tbsp olive oil, for frying

sea salt and freshly ground black pepper

SAUCE

1 tbsp olive oil

1 shallot, peeled and chopped

1 garlic clove, peeled and chopped

3 tbsp white wine

100ml (3½fl oz) double cream

3 tbsp coarse-grain mustard, e.g. Pommery or Gordons

2 tbsp chopped fresh dill

Trim the monkfish (*see* recipe introduction), then cut into medallions about 2.5cm (1in) thick. Season with a little salt and press each medallion lightly into the cracked pepper to coat. Place in the refrigerator.

To make the sauce, heat the oil in a frying pan, add the shallot and garlic and sauté for 3 minutes. Add the wine and cook until evaporated. Stir in the cream and bring to the boil, then add the mustard, dill and seasoning. Reduce the heat and keep warm.

Wipe out the pan with kitchen paper.

Heat the oil for frying until very hot, add the monkfish medallions and cook for about 2 minutes on each side until browned and just firm when pressed. Remove and drain on kitchen paper.

Place the medallions on four warmed plates and spoon the sauce around.

Serving note Serve with Bubble and Squeak Cakes (*see* page 140) and a salad of crisp mixed leaves.

Seafood Pot

One of my little 'cheats' is to dress up a carton of Campbell's Deliciously Good soup, which can keep for weeks without the need for refrigeration yet tastes as fresh and delicious as homemade. The carrot and coriander variety makes a great instant sauce for a seafood platter, spiked with some freshly roasted cumin seeds. You will need a selection – or mélange as chefs would term it – of neatly prepared fresh fish and seafood.

SERVES 2

4 king scallops with corals, prepared

1 tsp cumin seeds

2 tbsp olive oil

a knob of butter

1 red mullet fillet, about 125g (4½oz), halved

1 monkfish fillet, about 125g (4½oz), cut into 2 medallions

1 sea bass or brill fillet, about 125g (4½oz), halved

1 salmon fillet, about 125g (4½oz), halved

4 baby or 1 medium-sized squid, cut into rings

1 wedge of lemon, for squeezing

250ml (9fl oz) carton Campbell's Deliciously Good Carrot and Coriander Soup

1 tbsp chopped fresh coriander

sea salt and freshly ground black pepper

Check that the scallops have been thoroughly cleaned and remove any thin black threads. Pat dry with kitchen paper.

Heat a large, non-stick frying pan, add the cumin seeds and dry-roast for about 3–4 minutes, tossing in the pan. Tip straight into a pestle and mortar and grind until quite finely ground.

Add 1 tbsp of the oil and the butter to the pan. When it is hot, add the fish and fry quickly until just cooked. The flesh of the fish should be well browned and the skin crispy.

Heat a griddle pan and add the remaining oil. Add the scallops and squid and cook quickly – squid must not be overcooked or they will be tough.

Remove the fish and seafood to a dish to keep warm. Season well and squeeze over a little lemon juice.

Pour the soup into the pan and add the ground cumin. Heat until gently bubbling and continue to simmer for about 2 minutes. Pour into warmed shallow soup bowls. Arrange the fish and seafood on top and scatter over the coriander. Serve immediately.

Red Mullet with Deep-fried Rocket and Toasted Sesame Seeds

Most fish, including red mullet, are available all year round, but the best season for this particular fish is from June or July to September. Avoid small fish, which are fiddly to prepare and contain a lot of tiny bones. If you can't get larger fish, use salmon fillets instead as there really isn't much point in persevering with red mullet that are too tiny. Food fashions come and go. Although I've never been one to follow a trend slavishly, I do love deep-frying herbs and salad leaves as a garnish. Deep-fried rocket is an especial favourite. Serve the fish with plain boiled new potatoes. The simple flavours work together amazingly well. Alternatively, roast new potatoes in olive oil with some garlic cloves, thyme, and rock salt for about 45 minutes on a high heat.

SERVES 2

2 red mullet fillets (with skin on but no bones), about 175g (6oz) each

oil, for deep-frying

115g (4oz) rocket leaves

2 tbsp olive oil

25g (1oz) sesame seeds, toasted

sea salt and freshly ground black pepper

Place the red mullet fillets on a flat surface, skin side up, and with a sharp knife make about eight small slashes in the skin. Be careful not to cut through the whole width of the skin, but leave about 5mm (¼in) on either side of the fillet.

Heat the oil in a deep pan or fryer to a high heat. Don't wash the rocket, but place it in the fryer in two batches: this is to prevent the fat from overflowing as, when you add the rocket, it will bubble up, so be careful. Keep your eye on the rocket and remove from the fryer once the leaves go translucent. Don't overcook as the rocket will taste bitter; undercooking will prevent the leaves crisping up. Once you have removed them from the fryer, place on some kitchen paper to drain, and season with a little salt.

Heat a non-stick frying pan to a high heat on the stove with the olive oil. Season the mullet fillets, place in the pan, skin side down, and cook for about 2 minutes, until the skin is nice and crispy. Then turn them over and cook for about 1 minute.

Divide the crisp rocket between two plates. Place the red mullet fillets, skin side up, in the middle of the rocket, sprinkle with some of the toasted sesame seeds and serve.

Mullet on Smoky Red Pepper Salad

Brindisa imports the most divine ready-grilled and skinned baby red peppers from Spain, which I use in a quick dish of pan-fried red mullet served on a chicory-leaf salad. Tucked in between are shavings of sweet, tangy Parmesan and the whole plate is drizzled with a truffle-flavoured lemon-and-oil dressing.

SERVES 2

2 red mullet fillets (with skin on), about 200g (7oz) each

1 head of chicory, core removed and leaves separated

a good handful of rocket leaves

2 plum tomatoes, deseeded

25g (1oz) Parmesan

2 tbsp olive oil

4 small chargrilled red peppers in oil, drained

sea salt and freshly ground black pepper

DRESSING

4 tbsp olive oil

juice of 1 lemon

1 tbsp balsamic vinegar

1 small shallot, peeled and finely chopped

1 tsp truffle oil (optional, but effective)

Check the mullet for any stray bones by running your fingers along the flesh. If you feel any, pinch them out with your fingertips or use a pair of tweezers. Set the fish aside.

Tear the chicory leaves into bite-sized pieces and mix with the rocket in a bowl. Slice the tomatoes and add to the bowl with seasoning.

Whisk together all the ingredients for the dressing. Shave the Parmesan into slivers using a swivel vegetable peeler.

Heat the oil in a large frying pan, add the mullet, skin side down, and cook for about 5 minutes until the flesh feels just firm when pressed with the back of a fork. Carefully turn over with a fish slice, taking care not to damage the pretty pink skin. Cook the flesh side very briefly – 1 minute at the most.

Toss the salad with half the dressing. Divide between serving plates and place in the centre of each. Top with the Parmesan shavings, then 2 peppers each and finally crown with the mullet fillets, skin side up (the skin is so inviting, why not flaunt it?). Drizzle the remainder of the dressing around the plates and serve.

Whole sea bass is now as popular as salmon for serving at a summer party, although it is a bit more expensive. You can find farmed sea bass, flown in from the Mediterranean, but they may be smaller, in which case you will need two. Ask the fishmonger to scale the skin well. You can remove the head and fins, but the fish looks majestic intact. Roasting the limes alongside makes them more juicy and fragrant.

Sea Bass with Summer Herbs and Roasted Limes

SERVES 4–6

1 whole sea bass, about 1.3–1.8kg (3–4lb), scaled and gutted

100ml (3½fl oz) olive oil

3 large limes

3 tbsp chopped fresh mixed herbs, e.g. marjoram, parsley, basil, dill or oregano, plus a few whole sprigs to garnish (optional)

sea salt and freshly ground black pepper

Wash the fish thoroughly under cold running water, especially the body cavity, paying attention to rubbing out any clotted blood along the backbone. Pat dry with kitchen paper. Make slashes diagonally across the fish, about four to six in all, on both sides. Place the fish in a roasting pan and brush lightly with some of the oil.

Grate the zest of 1 lime and squeeze the juice. Mix with the chopped herbs and press the mixture into the slashes. Don't worry if it looks rather messy.

Preheat the oven to 200°C/400°F/gas mark 6.

Cut the other 2 limes in half and nestle alongside the fish. Season everything well and drizzle over the remaining oil.

Roast the fish in the oven, uncovered, for about 25–30 minutes until the flesh feels just firm when pressed. If you want to double-check that it is cooked, part some of the flesh down the backbone to see if it flakes.

Squeeze the juice from the roasted limes over the fish and serve on a platter with the pan juices trickled over. Use the squeezed lime shells as a garnish, along with some sprigs of the herbs you used, if desired.

A whole sea bass is a wonderful treat and really comes into its own when simply roasted with a handful of pine nuts, lots of garlic and lemon. And the pan juices provide the perfect sauce.

Sea Bass with Pine Nuts, Artichokes and Tomatoes

SERVES 4

1 whole sea bass, about 1kg (2lb 4oz), scaled and gutted

olive oil, for roasting

40g (1½oz) pine nuts

2 lemons, 1 thinly sliced, 1 squeezed for juice

6 ripe plum tomatoes, halved lengthways

6–10 garlic cloves (to taste), unpeeled

3 shallots, peeled and chopped

2 sprigs fresh thyme

200g (7oz) chargrilled artichokes in oil, drained and patted dry

2 tbsp chopped fresh parsley

100g (3½oz) rocket leaves

sea salt and freshly ground black pepper

Make sure the bass is thoroughly clean inside by washing under cold running water. Pat dry with kitchen paper.

Preheat the oven to 190°C/375°F/gas mark 5.

Rub the skin of the sea bass with a little olive oil and place in a roasting pan. Season well. Sprinkle over the pine nuts and lemon juice. Roast in the oven, uncovered, for about 20–25 minutes until the flesh feels quite firm and bouncy when pressed with the back of a fork. This indicates that it is almost cooked.

Meanwhile, place the tomatoes, cut side up, in a separate roasting pan. Trickle over a little olive oil, season well, then scatter over the garlic cloves, shallots and sprigs of thyme. Roast for 15 minutes until softened. Set aside to cool a little.

Slice and season the artichokes, then toss gently with the tomatoes.

Remove the fish from the oven and leave for 15 minutes before serving. Scoop off the pine nuts and gently mix with the tomatoes and artichokes. Cut the fish into fillets by inserting a sharp pointed knife into the backbone and loosening the flesh. Lift it from the bones, then pull away the whole skeleton from the tail to the head to reveal the underside fillet. Cut both fillets in half.

Squeeze the roasted garlic cloves from their skins and roughly chop. Add to the tomatoes and artichokes with the parsley and rocket leaves. Toss gently to mix.

Divide the salad between serving plates and place the fish on top. Season well, drizzle over any pan juices and serve.

Sprouting wheatgerm is a fantastic ingredient and is available in health food shops and some delicatessens; although, if it is unavailable, crushed canned chickpeas make a good alternative. In this recipe, the wheatgerm works well with Mediterranean vegetables as a salad and it's the perfect accompaniment to the sea bass.

Sea Bass with Sprouting Wheatgerm Salad

SERVES 2

125g (4½oz) sprouting wheatgerm

2 plum tomatoes, halved lengthways and seeded

1 shallot, peeled and finely chopped

1 fat garlic clove, peeled and chopped

1 tbsp black olives, pitted and chopped

2 pimientos (red peppers) in oil, well drained and chopped

1 tbsp chopped fresh basil

2 tbsp extra virgin olive oil

1 tbsp balsamic vinegar

2 sea bass fillets (with skin on), about 175g (6oz) each, and neatly trimmed

4 chargrilled artichokes in oil, well drained

1 tbsp chopped fresh parsley

juice of 1 lemon

sea salt and freshly ground black pepper

Place the wheatgerm in a pan, cover with cold water and bring to the boil. Reduce the heat and simmer gently, uncovered, for 45 minutes. Drain and set aside.

Cut the tomato halves into thin strips, then cut these into fine dice. Mix with the shallot, garlic, olives, pimientos and basil. Season well and toss with 1 tbsp of the oil and the vinegar. Set aside.

Heat a heavy-based, non-stick frying pan. Rub the bass skin with the remaining oil. When you feel a good heat rising from the pan, add the bass, skin side down, and cook for about 5 minutes until almost cooked. Turn over carefully to cook the other side. Season, remove from the pan and keep warm.

Thinly slice the artichokes, add to the pan and heat through for about 2 minutes. Transfer to two warmed serving plates.

Mix the cooked wheatgerm with the parsley, lemon juice and seasoning and spoon on top of the artichokes. Spoon the tomato and pimiento mixture around the edge and finally place a cooked sea bass fillet on the top. Serve immediately.

Smoked Mackerel Pâté with Chargrilled Courgettes

This is a no-fuss dish using bought pâté with the simple flavour of grilled courgettes. The courgettes must be grilled on a griddle pan – not under a grill – as this gives them essential colour, texture and flavour. Mackerel and courgettes are both underrated. Often it's the cheaper foods which taste the best; for example, rump steak compared with fillet steak.

SERVES 4

2 courgettes

1 tbsp olive oil, plus extra for drizzling

2 tbsp pesto

1 tbsp pine nuts, toasted

juice and grated zest of 1 lemon

250g (9oz) smoked mackerel pâté

few sprigs fresh basil

sea salt and freshly ground black pepper

Preheat a griddle pan to a high temperature.

Cut the courgettes in half, drizzle with olive oil and season with salt and pepper. Griddle the courgettes on both sides and leave to cool. Cut into bite-sized chunks.

Mix the pesto, pine nuts, lemon juice and zest and about 1 tbsp olive oil together, then season with salt and pepper. Leave to one side.

Place the chunks of courgette on a plate, and put a spoonful of pâté on top. Just before serving, add a spoonful of the pesto dressing. Garnish with sprigs of fresh basil around the edge.

Sardines are very underrated, but fresh sardines (and anchovies) are superb, not a bit like canned ones. Ask your fishmonger to gut and scale the fish and to remove the heads if you're put off by gleaming eyes staring at you. It also saves you a lot of time and mess. This is a dish I invented at home. It came about through a mistake while cooking. If most chefs are honest, that's how a lot of new dishes get created.

Grilled Sardines with a Raw Vegetable Salsa

SERVES 4

½ small carrot, finely chopped

½ red onion, peeled and finely chopped

1 red pepper, deseeded and finely chopped

½ red chilli, deseeded and finely chopped

1 garlic clove, peeled and finely chopped

12 fresh sardines, cleaned

2 tbsp olive oil, plus extra for drizzling

¼ small cucumber, finely chopped

juice and grated zest of 2 lemons

15g (½oz) fresh chives, chopped

15g (½oz) fresh coriander, chopped

sea salt and freshly ground black pepper

Prepare the vegetable dice and mix them together, apart from the cucumber.

Put the sardines on a tray, season them and drizzle with olive oil. Place under a preheated hot grill and cook for 3 minutes on one side. Turn them over and cook on the other side for another 2–3 minutes. Make sure the skin is good and crisp, as sardines are like mackerel: the skin must be crisp for maximum taste.

Add the cucumber dice and the juice and zest of the lemons to the diced vegetables, together with the olive oil and some seasoning. Place the mix in a pan and just warm through, or sling it in a microwave for a few seconds to warm it up. Don't overheat or the cucumber will go to mush.

Add the chopped herbs to the salsa, spoon over the hot sardines and serve.

Seared Salmon with Lime, Coriander and Tomato Salsa

As flavour is the most important aim in cooking, why do so many of us, chefs included, throw away half of the food in preparation – the skins of apples, for instance – which hold so much flavour?

SERVES 2

2 salmon fillets (with skin on, but no bones), about 175g (6oz) each

1 tbsp olive oil

sea salt and freshly ground black pepper

SALSA

1 red pepper

6 tomatoes

1 small red onion, peeled

½ red chilli, deseeded

15g (½oz) fresh coriander, chopped

juice and grated zest of 2 limes

Cut the pepper in half, remove the seeds and stalk, and cut the flesh into small dice. Chop the tomatoes into small dice, together with the red onion and chilli. Mix with the pepper dice.

Season the salmon and cook in the oil, skin side down, turning only once to stop it from breaking up. This should take no longer than 5–7 minutes.

Mix the chopped coriander and lime zest and juice into the pepper and tomato. Season well.

Place the salmon on plates with the salsa to one side and serve.

Salmon with Red Onion Pickle

Chargrilled salmon is always well received, and it is one of the most versatile fish, suiting a wide assortment of flavours. Here I match it with a rich red onion relish swirled with a really unusual vinegar – fig balsamic, a syrupy liquid made by steeping figs in a Californian balsamic wine vinegar. Don't expect a thin liquid; it has the consistency of a coulis. Other flavours in this range of extraordinary vinegars include blackcurrant and cherry. The whole dish has a taste of Scarborough Beach meets the Italian Riviera!

SERVES 4

½ cucumber

4 salmon fillets (with skin on), about 150g (5½oz) each

2 ripe tomatoes, halved, deseeded and finely chopped

4 tbsp fig balsamic vinegar

sprigs fresh chervil, to garnish (optional)

sea salt and freshly ground black pepper

RED ONION PICKLE

5 tbsp olive oil, plus extra for brushing

4 red onions, peeled and thinly sliced

2 fat garlic cloves, peeled and crushed

4 tbsp red wine

5 tbsp balsamic vinegar

1 sprig fresh thyme

2 tbsp caster sugar

2 tbsp chopped fresh parsley

To make the 'pickle', heat 4 tbsp of the oil in a saucepan, add the onions and garlic and sauté gently for about 5 minutes. Add the wine, vinegar, thyme and sugar.

Bring to the boil, then reduce the heat, cover and gently simmer for about 20 minutes. Uncover and continue cooking, stirring occasionally, until the liquid has evaporated away and the onions are meltingly soft. Stir in the parsley, set aside and leave to cool.

Meanwhile, halve the cucumber lengthways and scoop out the seeds. Cut the flesh into 4cm (1½in) batons. (If you have a chef's turning knife, you might like to try your hand at 'turning' them into barrel shapes.) Heat the remaining oil in a small saucepan, add the cucumber and sauté gently for about 5 minutes until hot and just soft. Season and set aside.

Season the salmon. Brush a heavy-based, ridged griddle pan with a light film of oil. Heat until very hot, add the salmon steaks, skin side down, and cook for about 4 minutes. Turn over carefully and cook the other side for about 2–3 minutes.

Spoon some of the pickle in the centre of warmed dinner plates, slide a salmon fillet on top, skin side up, and scatter around the cucumber batons and chopped tomatoes. Drizzle 1 tbsp fig balsamic vinegar per serving around the cucumber and tomatoes and over the salmon. Garnish with the chervil sprigs (if using) and serve.

Serving note New potatoes are the best accompaniment.

Champ is simply creamy mashed potatoes with the addition of chopped spring onions. To make it extra special, I serve it with a nicely cooked fish fillet and a quick sauce of wilted wild garlic. I appreciate that wild garlic is not readily on sale except in a few highly specialized country greengrocers. But in many parts of the country it grows in abundance along shady lanes and in woodlands in early summer. You cannot fail to notice it – the pungency wafts towards you well before you spot the lush green leaves and small white flowers. Out of season, use shredded young spinach leaves.

Salmon with Wild Garlic Sauce and Champ

SERVES 4

500g (1lb 2oz) large new potatoes, scrubbed to remove skin

100ml (3½fl oz) milk

40g (1½oz) butter

4–6 spring onions, chopped

1 tbsp olive oil

4 salmon fillets, about 125g (4½oz) each, skinned

5 tbsp Noilly Prat

200ml (7fl oz) single cream

2 garlic cloves, peeled and crushed

a small handful of wild garlic leaves or baby spinach leaves, roughly shredded

sea salt and freshly ground black pepper

Boil the potatoes in a saucepan of lightly salted water for about 12 minutes until just tender. Drain well and return to the pan to dry off a little over the lingering heat.

Meanwhile, place the milk in a saucepan and heat until on the point of boiling. Heat half the butter in a frying pan, add the spring onions and sauté for 1–2 minutes. Using a fork, mash the potatoes, gradually working in the hot milk, until you have a smooth paste. You may not need all the milk – it depends on the variety of potato. Beat the spring onions into the potato, season well and keep warm.

Heat the remaining butter with the oil in a large frying pan. Season the fish, add to the pan and fry for about 2 minutes on each side, or longer for thicker-cut fillets, until just firm.

Remove the salmon from the pan and keep warm. Add the Noilly Prat to the pan and allow to bubble for 1–2 minutes, then add the cream and crushed garlic and cook for about 2 minutes until reduced by about a third.

Season the sauce, then add the shredded wild garlic leaves or spinach and cook for a few seconds until wilted.

To serve, spoon the champ on to the centre of warmed serving plates. Place a fish fillet on top and spoon over the wild garlic sauce.

Serving note I like to garnish this dish with some deep-fried enoki mushrooms – long, spindly fungi that grow in clumps. They are sometimes available from larger supermarkets.

Chargrilled Smoked Salmon with Rocket and Parmesan

Smoked salmon on its own is superb, but as when added to scrambled eggs, cooked smoked salmon is divine. Here I've taken an unusual approach and chargrilled it in a griddle pan, which gives it great flavour. This dish could also be served as a light main course for two people.

SERVES 4

55g (2oz) Parmesan

4 tbsp olive oil, plus extra for drizzling

2 tbsp balsamic vinegar

200g (7oz) rocket leaves

225g (8oz) sliced smoked salmon

freshly ground black pepper

Using a potato peeler, shave all the cheese into thin strips, and set to one side.

Mix the olive oil and the vinegar together with some seasoning. Mix into the rocket leaves quickly and carefully, and place on the plates.

Heat a griddle pan to a high heat. Remove the salmon from the packet and fold each slice into three to make one thicker slice. Season with black pepper and drizzle on one side with a little olive oil.

When the pan is very hot, place the salmon on it, oiled side down, and leave for about 15 seconds. Turn it 90 degrees, cook for another 15 seconds, then remove. Do not turn it over: cook only on one side.

Sprinkle the rocket with the Parmesan shavings and place the salmon, charred side up, on the top. Serve immediately, ideally with a glass of chilled chardonnay.

Seared Tuna with Coriander Mash and Crispy Onions

It was only when I went diving in the Maldives that I truly appreciated how stunningly beautiful and enormous tuna are. I swam with about 80 yellowfin, some 30 dolphins and several barracuda in one dive. It was there, too, that I first experienced the taste of really fresh tuna. We barbecued it on the beach with fresh lime and coriander until still rare in the middle, and ate it off tin-lid plates sitting on the sand. Tuna must be as fresh as possible, and cooked with the minimum fuss to medium rare. Most supermarkets sell fresh tuna, but it is best to buy it cut to order from a fishmonger. It should be firm and a dark purple in colour.

SERVES 2

2 fresh tuna steaks, about 140g (5oz) each

4–6 tbsp olive oil, plus extra for drizzling

2 small white onions, peeled and sliced into rings

sea salt and freshly ground black pepper

CORIANDER MASH

2 estima potatoes

45g (½oz) fresh coriander

1 garlic clove, peeled

juice and zest of 2 limes

50ml (2fl oz) olive oil

75ml (2½fl oz) milk, hot

Peel and quarter the potatoes and place them in a saucepan. Cover with water, add a good pinch of salt and bring to the boil. Cook until tender, then drain and leave to one side.

Place most of the coriander, the garlic and half the juice and zest of the limes into a blender. Blend with the olive oil to achieve a pesto-like purée. Season well and leave to one side.

Season the tuna steaks well and place on a hot griddle pan with a drizzle of olive oil. Cook for about 2 minutes on each side so that they are nice and pink.

While the fish is cooking, mash the potatoes by hand with the milk. Mix in the coriander purée, season with salt and pepper and leave to one side.

In a hot pan, in the olive oil, fry the onion rings until golden brown and crisp; a few minutes. When they are ready, remove from the pan and place on kitchen paper to drain.

To serve, arrange the mash in the centre of two plates, with the tuna on the side. Add the crispy onions, and sprinkle over the remaining lime zest and juice, coriander leaves and a little pepper. Drizzle with olive oil and serve immediately.

Tip When making mashed potatoes, always leave the drained potatoes to one side for a few minutes before mashing them. This allows any moisture to evaporate. If the potatoes are puréed too soon, the water clinging to them will make the mash runny.

Another top mash tip is to use estima potatoes, which are floury rather than waxy and make for a very creamy purée. Using warm liquid helps to prevent lumps forming while the potatoes are being puréed.

Basil Oil Tuna with Deep-fried Garlic

Californian chefs evolved a unique style by simply not imposing any constraints on their cooking. Consequently, they excel at mixing and matching the very best of every cuisine. This recipe is based on a dish I ate in the buzzy Napa Valley restaurant of chef Michael Chiarello called Tra Vigne. With over 250 covers for lunch and dinner and a real wood-burning oven at the heart of the restaurant, the atmosphere was really jumpin'. You'll need a very fresh loin of tuna for this recipe since it is served raw, sliced wafer thin.

SERVES 4

a long fillet of tuna loin, about 350g (12oz) (*see* Ingredients notes)

5 tbsp basil oil (*see* Ingredients notes)

2 large lemons

groundnut oil, for frying

5 fat garlic cloves, peeled and sliced wafer thin

3 shallots, sliced wafer thin

100g (3½oz) rocket leaves

sea salt and freshly ground black pepper

Trim the tuna to form a neat log shape and wrap tightly in clingfilm. Place in the freezer for about 1 hour until firm. This makes for easier slicing.

Slice the ice-cold tuna as thinly as possible and lay out on four serving plates, as you would slices of smoked salmon. Brush all over with half the basil oil, season and place in the refrigerator for 30 minutes to absorb the flavour.

Meanwhile, peel one of the lemons and remove the white pith. Cut between the membranes to remove the segments. Squeeze the juice from the other lemon. Set the segments and juice aside.

Heat the groundnut oil to a depth of 3cm (1¼in) in a frying pan. When it is hot but not smoking, add the garlic and shallots and deep-fry for 1–2 minutes until pale golden brown and crisp. Drain on kitchen paper and set aside.

Dress the rocket leaves with the remaining basil oil, then toss with the lemon juice and seasoning.

Place the dressed rocket leaves and lemon segments on the edge of each plate with the tuna, then scatter over the crispy garlic and shallots. Serve immediately.

Ingredients notes Use yellowfin tuna for the best flavour. For the dressing, I use Consozio Basil Oil as made by Chef Chiarello himself.

Serving note Thinly sliced rye bread makes an excellent accompaniment for this dish.

Much was made a few years ago of a new supergrain called quinoa (pronounced 'keenwa'), said to be an ancient food of the Incas. Higher in protein than other grains, it also happens to taste good when tossed with ingredients such as lime, olives, garlic and chilli. I like to serve it with a juicy cooked tuna steak, but other seafood or pan-fried chicken would be equally fine.

Seared Tuna with Quinoa and Kalamata Olives

SERVES 4

200g (7oz) quinoa

juice and grated zest of 1 lime

1 large red chilli, deseeded and chopped

1 garlic clove, peeled and crushed

3 tbsp kalamata olives, pitted and chopped

2 tbsp deseeded and chopped cucumber

4 tbsp chopped fresh mixed herbs, e.g. parsley, dill or chervil

4 tbsp olive oil

1 plum tomato, deseeded and finely chopped

3 tbsp red wine vinegar

4 tuna steaks, about 125g (4½oz) each

sea salt and freshly ground black pepper

Rinse the quinoa well in cold running water to remove any bitterness. Drain well. Place in a saucepan of cold water. Bring to the boil, then reduce the heat, cover and simmer for about 15 minutes until the grains are tender and translucent. Drain to remove any remaining liquid and return to the pan. Stir in the lime juice and zest, chilli, garlic, olives, cucumber, half the herbs and 1 tbsp of the oil. Season well and set aside.

Mix the remaining herbs with the chopped tomato, 2 tbsp of the oil, the vinegar and seasoning for the dressing. Set aside.

Rub the remaining oil over the tuna steaks and season. Heat a ridged griddle pan or heavy-based frying pan until you feel a good heat rising. Add the tuna steaks and cook for about 2 minutes on each side if you like your tuna pink in the middle, or for a few minutes longer for medium-cooked steaks.

Reheat the quinoa and divide between warmed serving plates. Top with the tuna steaks and spoon the dressing either over the top of the steaks or around the edge before serving.

Ingredients note Purple kalamata olives from Greece are regarded by some gourmets as probably the best in the world. They are certainly among the largest!

When I was about eight years old, my family had a holiday house in a small and beautiful village called Robin Hood's Bay near Whitby in North Yorkshire. Whenever we visited Whitby, all the other kids would either climb the 150 steps to the castle or spend their pocket money at the amusements. I would spend the entire day watching the fishing boats go in and out of the harbour, and would invariably park myself next to the open window of a fish smokery. My mum would object vociferously as we travelled back in the car: I used to smell like an old kipper. Jugged kippers aren't at all like jugged hare. They are called this only because they are heated up in a jug. This is a very quick and simple dish that should take only a few minutes.

Jugged Fresh Kippers with Cider Butter and Lime

SERVES 2

2 fresh kippers

100g (3½oz) butter, softened

3 tbsp chopped fresh parsley

¼ apple, grated

50ml (2fl oz) cider

juice and grated zest of 1 lime

Place the kippers in a tall jug with the tails sticking out of the top, and carefully pour boiling water into the jug, up to the top.

Place the softened butter in a bowl and mix first with the chopped parsley, then more slowly with the grated apple and cider. Leave to one side.

After the kippers have been in the water for about 2–3 minutes, pour off the water and place them first on kitchen paper to dry and then on plates.

Put half the butter on to each kipper along with the juice and zest of the lime. Eat as is, or with some sliced bread.

shellfish

A quick, no-frills snack or starter. Buy large prawns, usually available from supermarket fish counters. They are expensive, but are normally fresh rather than frozen. Because of their size, they are easier to pick up and dip into the mayonnaise. Rocket is very popular, as it should be, because it tastes great. Try to buy rocket in bunches from a greengrocer as it's much cheaper than buying it in packets at a supermarket.

Jumbo Prawns with Rocket Mayonnaise

SERVES 2

10 large cooked prawns

15g (½oz) fresh basil

85g (3oz) rocket leaves

juice of 1 lime

200ml (7fl oz) mayonnaise

sea salt and freshly ground black pepper

Prepare the prawns by peeling them from the tail up to the head. Try to keep the head attached as they look better when kept whole.

In a food processor, purée half the basil and all the rocket together until smooth. Add the lime juice and mix into the mayonnaise. Season well with salt and pepper and place into a bowl on a serving dish.

Place the prawns around the bowl, and garnish with the rest of the fresh basil in sprigs.

Crab Cakes

Fish cakes are versatile little things. They can be homely and simple or wildly sophisticated. They can also be very dry and stodgy, but not this recipe. Make them ahead and serve with a homemade relish, such as my Cucumber and Green Pepper Relish, (see page 287), or buy a good-quality relish if you haven't the time or inclination. If you can't find fresh dressed crab meat, frozen or a superior branded can of white meat will do.

SERVES 4

500g (1lb 2oz) king edward potatoes, cut into large, evenly sized chunks

25g (1oz) butter

2 tbsp double cream

1 tsp mild or medium-strength curry powder

2 tbsp chopped fresh coriander

1 large fresh green chilli, deseeded and finely chopped

1 tbsp grated red onion

500g (1lb 2oz) flaked crab meat, preferably white meat but a mixture of white and brown will do, thawed well if frozen

2–3 tbsp plain flour, seasoned

2 free-range eggs, beaten

100g (3½oz) dried breadcrumbs (uncoloured)

corn or sunflower oil, for deep-frying

sea salt and freshly ground black pepper

Boil the potatoes in a saucepan of lightly salted water for about 15 minutes until tender. Drain well, then return to the pan. Mash with a fork or potato masher until smooth, beating in the butter, cream, curry powder, coriander, chilli, onion and lots of seasoning. Leave to cool completely.

Meanwhile, check the crab meat carefully for any flecks of shell and discard. Mix the crab meat with the potato mixture, then shape into 8 neat round patties. If the mixture sticks to your hands, simply dip them in cold water.

To coat the crab cakes in breadcrumbs requires a methodical approach. Complete each of the three stages for all the cakes before moving on to the next. That way, you won't get too messy. So, first toss each cake in seasoned flour, shake well and place on a plate.

Beat the eggs in a wide shallow bowl, then dip each cake into the egg to coat evenly.

Place the breadcrumbs in another wide shallow bowl and toss each cake in the crumbs in turn, pressing the crumbs on to the eggy surface to coat evenly. Shake off any excess and place the cakes on a plate. Chill in the refrigerator for about 30 minutes to 'set' the crumbs.

Heat oil to a depth of 1cm (½in) in a wide shallow frying pan until you feel a good heat rising. Carefully slide in the crab cakes using a fish slice. Cook for about 3 minutes until crisp and golden brown on the underside, then carefully turn and cook the other side. Remove and place on kitchen paper. (If you have a medium-sized frying pan, you may find it best to fry the crab cakes in two batches.) Serve piping hot. However, if not serving immediately, place uncovered in a warm oven so that the coating stays crisp.

Tempura Squid with Pepperonella

This dish sounds more complicated than it actually is. Pepperonella, which is made with fresh tomatoes and freshly roasted peppers, can be bought ready-made in jars, which saves a lot of hassle and time and tastes fine. The squid must be cleaned and prepared properly; ask the fishmonger to do this. Squid should be cooked quickly on a high heat, only until golden brown, otherwise it will probably be tough.

SERVES 4

650g (1lb 7oz) prepared squid (body only)

oil, for deep-frying

30g (½oz) fresh mint, chopped

1 x 200g jar pepperonella (or some Roasted Peppers, *see* page 174)

BATTER
225g (8oz) plain flour

2 egg yolks

400ml (14fl oz) water

sea salt and freshly ground black pepper

Cut the squid across the body into rings.

Make the batter by mixing the flour, egg yolks and water together with a little salt and pepper. It should be quite thin. Don't worry if it's lumpy.

Heat the oil in a deep pan or fryer to a moderate to high heat. Dip the squid rings in the batter, then place in the hot oil and cook until golden brown: a few minutes only. Drain on kitchen paper and season with a little salt.

Serve in a pile with chopped mint on the top and the pepperonella on one side.

Parmesan Grilled Lobster with a Lime and Chilli Mayonnaise and Chips

This dish, although impressive, is quick and easy. Basically it's just upmarket fish and chips – but on a lottery-winning scale. Although pre-cooked lobster is available, almost all year round, from most supermarkets, it tastes much better bought fresh and alive from a fishmongers. It is normally cooked for about 18–20 minutes per kg (8–9 minutes per lb) in boiling water.

SERVES 2

1 x 675g (1lb 8oz) cooked lobster

2 tbsp mild curry powder

15g (½oz) fresh basil, chopped

8 tbsp double cream

40g (1½oz) Parmesan, grated

2 large estima potatoes

oil, for deep-frying

sea salt and freshly ground black pepper

LIME AND CHILLI MAYONNAISE

150ml (¼ pint) mayonnaise

juice and grated zest of 1 lime

½ large red chilli, deseeded and finely diced

Prepare the lobster by cutting it in half lengthways with a sharp knife. Take the legs off and, with a pair of nutcrackers or lobster crackers, open them up to remove the flesh. Place the flesh in a bowl. Remove the tail meat, slice and add to the claw meat. Remove the head meat and throw this away. Season the meat with salt, pepper and curry powder to taste, plus the chopped basil.

Place the meat back in the shells and pour the cream over. Top with the grated Parmesan and leave to one side.

Mix the mayonnaise in a bowl with the lime juice, zest and diced chilli.

Heat the oil in a deep pan or fryer to a high heat. Cut the potatoes into large chips and cook for about 6–8 minutes until golden brown.

Meanwhile, place the lobster under a preheated grill to colour the cheese.

Remove the lobster from the grill and place on two plates. Serve the chips and the mayonnaise on the side.

Seared Scallop and Coriander Salad with a Lime and Red Pepper Dressing

Basically there are two types of scallop – queens and kings – and there is a great difference between them. King scallops are larger than queens and are diver-caught. They provide a much more substantial piece of meat, but at a price. Steer clear of queens which are small, and after cooking end up looking like buttons. And never – repeat never – buy scallops that have been frozen: when defrosted and cooked they lose all their flavour, leaving a pan full of defrosted water to boot.

SERVES 2

1 red pepper

6 tbsp extra virgin olive oil, plus extra for drizzling

juice and grated zest of 2 limes

30g (½oz) fresh coriander, half of it chopped

1 tbsp chopped red onion

6 large king scallops with corals, prepared

1 x 250g (9oz) bag prewashed mixed salad leaves

sea salt and freshly ground black pepper

Preheat the oven to 200°C/400°F/gas mark 6.

Cut the pepper in half, discard the seeds and stalk, and place in an ovenproof dish. Season with salt and pepper, drizzle with olive oil and place in the oven for 15 minutes until the skin has browned. Remove from the oven and, while the pepper is hot, place in a bowl, quickly cover with clingfilm and leave to go cold. When it is cold, remove and discard the skin.

For the dressing, cut the pepper flesh into small dice and place in a bowl with the lime juice and zest. Add the olive oil with the chopped coriander and onion. Season and leave to one side.

Remove any black threads or sand from the scallops, but do not wash them. Heat a frying pan until very hot. Season the scallops with salt and pepper, place in the very hot pan and dry-fry on both sides for 30 seconds or until just cooked.

Combine half the dressing with the salad leaves and remaining coriander leaves, and pile high on two plates. Put the scallops on top of the salad. Finish the dish by drizzling the remaining dressing around the edge, and serve.

Tip Any salad leaves would do, but the prewashed bags are handy. The Continental selections normally contain a blend of frisée, radicchio and lollo rosso, while the Italian ones add rocket and herbs.

pasta, rice & gnocchi

Linguine with Roast Figs and Herbs

It has been fashionable recently to make your own pasta, supposedly like the Italians themselves. But anyone who has worked in good Italian kitchens knows that a lot of them use good-quality dried pastas, not fresh. The mixture of textures and flavours here is unusual, and very sexy. You could add toasted walnuts, almonds, pistachios or pine kernels for additional texture and sex appeal. This dish should only be made with fresh figs, not canned or dried.

SERVES 4

4 large fresh figs

8 slices speck bacon (or prosciutto or Parma ham)

2 shallots, peeled and chopped

2 garlic cloves, peeled and chopped

1 tbsp olive oil, plus extra for cooking the pasta

100ml (3½fl oz) white wine

200g (7oz) Dolcelatte cheese

300ml (½pint) double cream

2 large sprigs fresh mint, chopped

15g (½oz) fresh basil, chopped

15g (½oz) fresh chives, chopped

400g (14oz) linguine

40g (1½oz) Parmesan, freshly grated

sea salt and freshly ground black pepper

Preheat the oven to 230°C/450°F/gas mark 8.

Wrap the figs in the speck bacon, and secure with wooden cocktail sticks. Bake in the oven for about 5–6 minutes, until the bacon is nice and crisp.

Meanwhile, sweat the shallots and garlic in the olive oil for a few minutes, then add the white wine. Boil to reduce by half, then add the cheese and cream. Reduce until slightly thickened, but do not boil, or the mixture will split because of the fat in the cheese. Season with salt and pepper and add some of the herbs.

Cook the pasta in a generous amount of boiling salted water, with a little oil in it, following the timing given on the packet, usually about 6–8 minutes.

Combine the pasta and sauce, divide between plates and garnish with the figs and the remaining fresh herbs. Top with the freshly grated Parmesan before serving.

Penne Carbonara

Opinions differ about the origins of this hip classic. Some say it was a supper dish enjoyed by charcoal burners in Rome, other stories link it to American GIs in Italy at the end of the Second World War. Wherever it came from, a good carbonara needs crisp pancetta and matured fresh Parmigiano Reggiano, and is best freshly made in the pan. At all costs, avoid the glutinous sauces sold in jars under the same name.

SERVES 2 AS A MAIN COURSE, 4 AS A STARTER

250g (9oz) fresh or dried penne

2 tbsp olive oil

175g (6oz) pancetta, thinly sliced

5 free-range egg yolks

150ml (¼ pint) double cream

100g (3½oz) Parmesan, half finely grated, half as shavings

3–4 tbsp chopped fresh parsley

sea salt and freshly ground black pepper

Boil the penne in a large saucepan of lightly salted boiling water for about 8–10 minutes, or according to the packet instructions, until just tender. Rinse quickly under cold water to stop the cooking process.

Meanwhile, heat 1 tbsp of the oil in a frying pan, add the pancetta and fry until crisp.

In a large bowl, beat the egg yolks with the cream and grated Parmesan. Season well with pepper (hold back the salt until the end of the preparation); add the chopped parsley.

When the pasta is cooked, drain and toss immediately with the sauce in the bowl, together with the remaining oil and the pancetta. Check the seasoning and serve in a warmed bowl. Top with shavings of Parmesan.

There are a number of Spanish chorizo sausages on sale, which make for good alfresco eating. My favourites are the large paprika-flavoured picante ones. Meaty and tasty, they are good cut into slices and quickly pan-fried, ready to be tossed with pasta. This recipe works well with any pasta shapes.

Pesto Pasta with Picante Chorizo and Artichokes

SERVES 4

500g (1lb 2oz) dried pasta shapes (any variety of a quality brand)

200g (7oz) picante chorizo, sliced

1 x 200g jar artichoke hearts in oil, drained and oil reserved

3 tbsp freshly made pesto (*see* page 110)

50g (1¾oz) Parmesan

sea salt and freshly ground black pepper

Cook the pasta in a large saucepan of lightly salted boiling water, according to the packet instructions, until just tender. Drain, reserving a cup of the cooking water.

Meanwhile, heat a non-stick frying pan or a ridged griddle pan until you feel a good heat rising. Add the chorizo slices and cook for about 5 minutes, turning, until crisp on both sides.

Toss the pasta with the oil from the artichokes and season well. Cut the artichokes into wedges and add with the pesto to the chorizo in the pan to warm through. Toss the pasta in the mixture. If you like a slightly thinner sauce, add the cup of pasta cooking water.

Season the pasta and tip into a large warmed serving bowl. Shave the Parmesan thinly using a swivel vegetable peeler and scatter over the pasta. Serve immediately.

Pasta with Pesto

I don't always suggest making pesto, but with a bought brand of pesto this dish is like fish and chips without the newspaper: it just doesn't taste the same.

SERVES 4

400g (14oz) good-quality dried penne

85g (3oz) Parmesan, made into shavings

sea salt and freshly ground black pepper

BASIL PESTO

55g (2oz) fresh basil

1 garlic clove, peeled

2 canned anchovy fillets

1 tbsp pine kernels, toasted

6 tbsp olive oil

25g (1oz) Parmesan, freshly grated

sprigs of fresh basil (optional)

Cook the penne in a generous amount of boiling salted water following the timing given on the packet, usually about 10–12 minutes.

Meanwhile, place the basil, garlic, anchovy fillets, pine kernels, olive oil and grated cheese in a blender. Purée the mix and season with salt and pepper. Add more oil if necessary – enough to create a thickish purée – and remove from the blender.

Drain the pasta well and place into a bowl with some ground black pepper and salt. Mix the pesto through it. Place in a large bowl and sprinkle the Parmesan shavings on top to serve. You could also top it with some freshly ripped-up leaves of basil.

A spicy dried pork sausage, chorizo looks like a little salami. It needs infusing first, to bring out the full flavour, and shouldn't really be eaten raw. Some supermarkets and delicatessens, however, offer a larger picante version, usually sold thinly sliced.

Pasta with Chorizo Sausage, Tomato and Rocket

SERVES 2

1 very small chorizo sausage, thinly sliced

2 garlic cloves, peeled and chopped

2 tbsp olive oil

1 x 600g can plum tomatoes

200g (7oz) good-quality dried penne

55g (2oz) rocket leaves

20g (¾oz) fresh flat-leaf parsley, roughly chopped

1 x 150g (5½oz) ball of buffalo mozzarella cheese, grated

sea salt and freshly ground black pepper

In a pan heat the olive oil, add the chorizo and garlic, and cook for a few minutes. Add the can of tomatoes, bring to the boil, and cook for about 10 minutes. This is important as it draws out the flavour of the sausage.

Cook the pasta in a generous amount of boiling salted water following the timing given on the packet, usually about 10–12 minutes. Drain well.

Rip the rocket leaves in half and add to the sauce together with three-quarters of the parsley. Season well. Mix the sauce and pasta together and place in a dish. Top with the grated mozzarella and the rest of the parsley, and serve.

Tortellini in a Cèpes Sauce

There's a good range of tortellini – those stuffed morsels of pasta in a range of flavours and colours – to be found in delis, both fresh and dried. I prefer chicken or salmon tortellini, but you could use any of the cheese or spinach varieties in this recipe. Cèpes (called *porcini* in Italy) are a species of wild mushroom, the *Boletus edulis*, and a cook's very good friend. Sold dried in handy packs, they keep almost indefinitely, yet, when soaked, yield a great flavour. You can use the soaking broth, too, as an almost instant stock.

SERVES 4

40g (1½oz) dried cèpes or *porcini* pieces

300ml (½ pint) boiling water

1 tbsp olive oil

2 shallots, peeled and chopped

2 garlic cloves, peeled and crushed

2 tbsp brandy

100ml (3½fl oz) muscat or other sweet white wine

250ml (9fl oz) double cream

400g (14oz) tortellini with chicken, fish, cheese or spinach filling, fresh or dried

4 tbsp chopped fresh herbs, e.g. dill, parsley or chervil, plus a few whole sprigs to garnish

a good knob of butter

2–3 tsp truffle oil (*see* Ingredients note)

sea salt and freshly ground black pepper

Place the dried cèpes in a bowl and pour over the boiling water just to cover. Cover the bowl and leave for 5 minutes. Drain, but reserve the soaking liquid. Slice the cèpes if large and set aside.

Heat the oil in a frying pan, add the shallots and garlic and sauté for about 5 minutes until softened. Stir in the brandy and wine. Bring to the boil and cook until reduced by half.

Add about half the reserved soaking liquid from the cèpes and the cream. Bring to the boil, stir in the cèpes and season well. Reduce the heat and simmer for about 5 minutes.

Cook the tortellini in boiling water according to the packet instructions until just tender. Drain well. Toss with the sauce together with the chopped herbs and butter.

Divide the pasta between warmed plates and trickle over the truffle oil. Serve garnished with a few herb sprigs.

Ingredients note A tip about truffle oil – buy the most concentrated you can. It may be expensive, but the pronounced flavour makes such a difference to a dish.

Serving note Sometimes I serve this pasta dish with neat fillets of pan-fried red mullet on top.

It is always worth buying the best pasta you can afford. You will be rewarded in flavour and texture. Generally speaking, I would suggest you steer clear of multi-coloured gimmicky-shaped pasta, but there are a few varieties that I consider to be exceptions to the rule. One of these is ferrazzudi di caladria – huge tubes of subtly coloured pasta. If you can't find this particular pasta, large rigatoni tubes would do, or even flat, thick pappardelle 'noodles'. This dish makes an excellent light summer-style lunch.

Lemon-dressed Pasta with Chargrilled Salmon

SERVES 4

500g (1lb 2oz) good-quality pasta tubes, e.g. ferrazzudi di caladria, giant rigatoni or flat pappardelle

4 salmon escalopes or fillets, about 100g (3½oz) each, skin removed

3 tbsp olive oil

juice and grated zest of 1 large lemon

50g (1¾oz) butter

3–4 tbsp double cream or crème fraîche

4 tbsp chopped mixed fresh herbs, e.g. basil, parsley, oregano or dill

50g (1¾oz) Parmesan, freshly grated

sea salt and freshly ground black pepper

Cook the pasta in a large saucepan of lightly salted boiling water for about 10 minutes, or according to the packet instructions, until just tender. Drain and tip straight into a large bowl.

Brush the salmon lightly with 1 tbsp of the oil, season and set aside while you finish the pasta.

Add the lemon zest and juice to the pasta with the remaining oil, the butter, cream or crème fraîche, herbs, Parmesan and seasoning. Mix well and set aside.

Heat a ridged griddle pan until you feel a good heat rising, or preheat the grill until hot. Add the salmon escalopes or fillets to the griddle pan, or place under the grill, and cook for 2–3 minutes on each side. (They should be neatly marked with chargrilled ridges if cooked in the pan.) The flesh inside should be lightly pink. Divide the pasta between warmed wide shallow serving bowls or plates, top with the salmon and grind over some black pepper.

Fresh Leaf Pasta

This is a good bit of fun, and tasty as well – fresh herbs rolled into freshly made pasta. Making your own pasta is simple if you have one of those hand-cranked pasta machines. It helps too if you have the right sort of flour. A good deli that specialises in Italian foods will stock a flour called 00 or doppio zero (strong bread flour makes tough fresh pasta). Cut the pasta into small rounds or thick strips, or use in sheets for an elegant lasagne. You can make the pasta with whole leaf herbs, chopped herbs or, of course, with no herbs at all.

SERVES 2–3

275g (9½oz) pasta flour

1 tsp salt

1 tbsp olive oil

2 eggs, beaten, and 2 egg yolks

a selection of whole fresh herb leaves, e.g. thyme, sage, coriander or mint

butter and grated Parmesan, to serve

Put the flour and salt (and chopped herbs, if using instead of whole leaf) into a food processor. With the blades running, drop in the oil, yolks and most of the beaten eggs.

Blend the mixture until it just starts to stick together (you can check on this if you press a little together between your fingers). You may not need all the egg – it depends on the flour. If you use all the egg and it still seems a little dry, trickle in some cold water. Do not overbeat the dough; just pull it together into a ball.

Set up your pasta machine. Break off a lump of dough the size of a large walnut and, with the rollers set on the highest number, feed the dough through about five times.

Set the rollers to the next setting down and repeat. Repeat this until you reach the third thinnest setting. By now the dough will have become very smooth and elastic. Try to keep the edges as straight as possible.

Lay the dough sheet out on a lightly floured board, and if using whole herb leaves press them lightly on to the dough (*see* left).

Repeat with the remaining dough in stages. After rolling out the second sheet, place this on top of the first and press down. Feed this double sheet through the rollers again. Keep on rolling and pressing the leaves in until finished.

Cut the pasta into rounds or straight sheets and leave to dry on sheets of non-stick baking parchment.

Blanch in a large pan of salted boiling water for just 1–2 minutes until *al dente*.

Serve the pasta dressed with butter and grated Parmesan.

Tinned Tomato and Pesto Risotto

Tinned tomatoes are better than fresh for this risotto as they have a superior flavour once they are puréed. The colour is better too: bright red, rather than the pink of fresh tomatoes. Use a proper risotto rice, such as arborio or, better still, carnaroli which soaks up the liquid more. Never buy those coloured rices on offer in supermarkets. They're just a gimmick, and don't really taste of anything when cooked.

SERVES 4

4 x 400g tins plum tomatoes

½ red onion, peeled and finely diced

3 garlic cloves, peeled and finely diced

25g (1oz) butter

250g (9oz) risotto rice, such as arborio or carnaroli

115g (4oz) Parmesan

2 tbsp pesto

30g (½oz) fresh basil

olive oil, for drizzling

sea salt and freshly ground black pepper

Place the tomatoes and their juice in a blender and purée until smooth. Leave to one side.

Sauté the onion and garlic in the butter for a minute.

Add the rice to the onion, and continue cooking for a further minute, before adding three-quarters of the puréed tomatoes. Bring to the boil and gently simmer for about 15 minutes, stirring continuously to stop it burning. If the mix is getting too dry, add some of the remaining puréed tomatoes.

Using a swivel vegetable peeler, shave about a quarter of the Parmesan into shavings. Then grate the remainder.

Add the grated cheese to the rice along with some salt, lots of black pepper (which brings out the flavour of the tomato) and the pesto. Stir well. To finish, add the fresh basil leaves, just ripped up and mixed in.

Spoon into soup plates and garnish with the shavings of Parmesan and a drizzle of olive oil.

Tip Be careful when adding the tomato liquid to the rice. Because it's thicker than a traditional stock, you have to stir almost all the time to prevent the rice sticking and burning on the bottom of the pan. And don't add all the liquid at the same time because then the risotto could be too wet.

Crevettes have a wonderful flavour and are available from good fishmongers, but if you can't find them use fresh prawns instead. Asparagus is now available all year round and, although nothing is as good as the new English variety, imported asparagus is acceptable. It's important that everything is added separately and at the appropriate time, as it is all very easy to overcook.

Crevette, Asparagus and Red Pepper Risotto

SERVES 4

½ red onion, peeled and finely chopped

2 garlic cloves, peeled and finely chopped

2 tbsp olive oil

250g (9oz) risotto rice, such as arborio or carnaroli

600ml (1 pint) fresh fish stock

1 red pepper, deseeded and cut into large cubes

8 asparagus spears, trimmed

100ml (3½fl oz) double cream

85g (3oz) Parmesan, freshly grated

15g (½oz) fresh basil

10 large cooked crevettes, peeled

sea salt and freshly ground black pepper

a few shavings of Parmesan (optional)

In a large pan, cook the onion and garlic in the oil until they soften slightly.

Add the rice and cook for about 30 seconds, stirring, then add the stock and bring to the boil. Simmer for about 15 minutes until the rice is cooked and has a porridge-like consistency. Add the red pepper cubes to the rice about halfway through the cooking. Keep stirring to avoid sticking to the bottom of the pan. Stir the red pepper cubes into the rice about halfway through the cooking.

Meanwhile, cut the asparagus spears in half across. Place in boiling water and cook for a few minutes until just cooked but not soft. Drain well.

When the rice is cooked, add the cream and grated Parmesan. Chop up the asparagus bottoms (not the tips) and mix them in as well. Season with salt and pepper and finish with the ripped-up fresh basil leaves.

Place the risotto into bowls, and garnish with the asparagus tips and Parmesan shavings (if using).

Mussel and Artichoke Risotto

Both mussels and artichokes are warming wintry comfort foods, so this risotto is ideal for when you just want to curl up in front of an open fire. Cook the mussels first in a little wine and butter until they open, then pull out the meat from the shells. It takes just minutes to prepare.

SERVES 3–4

1kg (2lb 4oz) fresh mussels

3 garlic cloves, peeled and crushed

3 shallots or 1 onion, peeled and chopped

150ml (¼ pint) dry white wine

50g (1¾oz) butter

2 tbsp olive oil

400g (14oz) Jerusalem artichokes, peeled and finely chopped

250g (9oz) risotto rice, such as arborio or carnaroli

about 800ml (1 pint 7fl oz) fresh fish stock or chicken stock

2 tbsp mascarpone

3 tbsp freshly grated Parmesan

1 tbsp chopped fresh parsley

sea salt and freshly ground black pepper

Wash the mussels in cold water, then pull away the wispy 'beards'. Place the mussels in a large pan but discard any that are open. Add 1 of the crushed garlic cloves, 1 of the chopped shallots or one-third of the chopped onion, the wine and half the butter.

Cover with a tight lid and cook over a medium heat for about 7 minutes. Uncover, strain the juices into a jug and set aside. When the mussels are cool enough to handle, pull the meat from the shells and set aside. Discard any mussels that have not opened.

Heat the oil in a frying pan, add the remaining garlic, shallots or onion and the artichokes and gently sauté for about 5 minutes until softened.

Stir in the rice and cook for 1–2 minutes until lightly toasted, then pour in all the mussel juices. Bring to the boil, stirring, and cook for about 5 minutes until the liquid is absorbed, stirring frequently.

Heat the stock until simmering and add a quarter to the rice. Simmer, uncovered, until the stock is absorbed, stirring frequently. Add the remainder of the stock a ladleful at a time in the same way until all the stock is absorbed and the rice grains are plump and tender yet still retain a good 'bite'. This should take 15–18 minutes. You may not need all the stock.

Stir in the mussels, the remaining butter, the mascarpone, Parmesan and parsley. Season well and serve piping hot and creamy.

Smoked halibut has a lovely delicate texture and pretty golden and creamy-tasting flesh. It makes a good substitute for smoked salmon as a starter, or try it lightly chargrilled and served with a risotto cooked in the classic Milano style with saffron and Parmesan, below.

Charred Smoked Halibut and Saffron Risotto

SERVES 4

1 litre (1¾ pints) fresh fish stock

a good pinch or two of saffron strands (*see* Ingredients note)

1 tbsp olive oil, plus extra for brushing

25g (1oz) butter

2 shallots, peeled and finely chopped

2 garlic cloves, peeled and chopped

250g (9oz) risotto rice, such as arborio or carnaroli

250g (9oz) smoked halibut slices

1 tbsp chopped fresh dill

40g (1½oz) Parmesan, freshly grated

sea salt and freshly ground black pepper

Pour the stock into a saucepan and bring to the boil. Remove from the heat and add the saffron. Leave to infuse while you make the risotto.

Heat the oil with the butter in a frying pan, add the shallots and garlic and sauté for about 5 minutes until softened. Stir in the rice and cook for 1–2 minutes until the grains are lightly toasted.

Heat the stock until simmering and add a quarter to the rice. Simmer, uncovered, until the stock is absorbed, stirring frequently. Add the remainder of the stock a ladleful at a time in the same way until all the stock is absorbed and the rice grains are plump and tender yet still retain a good 'bite'. This should take 15–18 minutes. You may not need all the stock.

Meanwhile, heat a ridged griddle pan and brush lightly with a tiny amount of oil. When it is hot, lay the halibut slices in the pan and cook for 1–2 minutes until marked on only one side. Don't overcook.

Season the risotto to taste and stir in the dill. Spoon into warmed serving bowls and sprinkle over the Parmesan. Lay the halibut slices on top and serve immediately.

Ingredients note Buy a good-quality Spanish brand of saffron with a deep aroma. You need only a pinch or two to impart a fine flavour.

 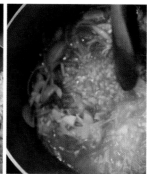 

Leek and Haddock Risotto

You need the real Finnan haddock with its creamy golden flesh for this recipe, not the bright yellow, artificially dyed fish that masquerades as smoked fish. Good smoked haddock is naturally coloured through the smoking process. The fish itself is plump and moist with a wonderful salty-sweet flavour from the simple, pure brine. I like to mix flakes of this fish into a leek risotto and, as a surprise, toss in a few cubes of crisply fried black pudding. Not only does it taste amazing – it looks so appealing. Try it for a light supper or unusual starter.

SERVES 4

1 tbsp olive oil

175g (6oz) good-quality black pudding, cut into thick slices, then into quarters

1 smoked Finnan haddock fillet, about 300–400g (10½–14oz)

25g (1oz) butter

3 shallots, peeled and chopped

2 garlic cloves, peeled and crushed

100ml (3½fl oz) dry white wine

250g (9oz) risotto rice, such as arborio or carnaroli

about 1.2 litres (2 pints) fresh fish or vegetable stock

2 medium leeks, thinly sliced

2–3 tbsp mascarpone or crème fraîche

freshly grated Parmesan (to taste)

chopped fresh parsley, to garnish

sea salt and freshly ground black pepper

Heat the oil in a wide shallow pan, add the chunks of black pudding and fry quickly for 1–2 minutes until crisp on the outside. Remove and set aside.

Skin the haddock and check carefully for any bones by running against the grain of the flesh with your fingertips. If you find any, pluck them out with your fingers or use a pair of tweezers. Cut the fish into 1cm (½in) chunks and set aside.

Heat the butter in the wide shallow pan, add the shallots and garlic and sauté for about 3 minutes until softened. Pour in the wine, bring to the boil and cook until reduced by half, stirring frequently. Stir in the rice and cook for 1–2 minutes until lightly toasted.

Heat the stock until simmering and add a quarter to the rice. Simmer, uncovered, until the stock is absorbed, stirring frequently.

Add a further quarter of the stock with the leeks and continue simmering until the liquid is absorbed, stirring occasionally. Add the fish, black pudding, the remaining stock and seasoning to taste. Continue simmering, stirring occasionally, until most of the stock is absorbed and the rice grains are plump and tender yet still retain a good 'bite'. The fish should be just cooked. The whole process should take 15–18 minutes.

Stir in the mascarpone or crème fraîche and Parmesan. Check the seasoning and serve immediately, sprinkled with chopped parsley.

Chicken Breasts with Asparagus and Muscat Risotto

Don't be afraid of cooking a savoury dish with a sweet wine. It blends perfectly with the other flavours, and it's certainly a good talking point at the table. Here, a sweet-and-savoury risotto is matched with pan-fried chicken breasts. Buy the best corn-fed organic chicken you can for the best flavour. You'll need to make the Muscat and Vanilla Syrup (see page 285) for this dish first, but it stores well for later use. You can, however, make the dish without it. A little basil oil is good for dressing the dish just before serving.

SERVES 4

25g (1oz) butter

2 tbsp olive oil

3–4 shallots, peeled and finely chopped

2 fat garlic cloves, peeled and crushed

200g (7oz) risotto rice, such as arborio or carnaroli

100ml (3½fl oz) muscat or other sweet dessert wine

700ml–1 litre (1¼–1¾ pints) fresh chicken stock

150g (5½oz) asparagus spears, stalks chopped and tips reserved

4 skinless, boneless chicken breasts, about 125g (4½oz) each

2 plum tomatoes, quartered, deseeded and finely chopped

2 tbsp chopped mixed fresh chervil and chives

5 tbsp Muscat and Vanilla Syrup (optional, *see* page 285)

1–2 tbsp mascarpone

basil oil, for drizzling

sprigs of fresh basil or parsley (optional)

sea salt and freshly ground black pepper

Heat the butter with the half the oil in a saucepan, add the shallots and garlic and sauté gently for about 5 minutes until softened.

Stir in the rice and cook for 1–2 minutes until lightly toasted. Add the wine, bring to the boil, stirring, and cook for about 5 minutes until the liquid is absorbed, stirring frequently.

Heat the stock until simmering and add a quarter to the rice. Simmer, uncovered, until the stock is absorbed, stirring frequently. Add the chopped asparagus stalks with a ladleful of stock. Continue simmering, stirring occasionally, until the stock is absorbed. Add the remaining stock a ladleful at a time in the same way until all the stock is absorbed and the rice grains are plump and tender yet still retain a good 'bite'. This should take 15–18 minutes.

Meanwhile, about 10 minutes before the end of the cooking time for the risotto, heat a frying pan until you feel a good heat rising. Add the remaining oil, then the chicken breasts and sauté for about 3–5 minutes on each side, depending on their thickness. They should feel firm when pressed with the back of a fork. Season as they cook.

When the risotto is nearly ready, stir in the asparagus tips, chopped tomatoes, herbs, 1 tbsp of the Muscat and Vanilla Syrup (if using) and mascarpone. Mix well and cook gently for 2 minutes. Season to taste.

Divide the risotto between warmed serving plates. Slice each chicken breast into medallions and arrange on top of the risotto. Drizzle the remaining Muscat and Vanilla Syrup (if using) around each plate and trickle over a few drops of basil oil. Garnish with basil or parsley sprigs (if using) and serve.

Grilled Gravadlax with Pesto Gnocchi

This is so easy to make, it's almost embarrassing. You can pick up the ingredients from your neighbourhood deli on your way home from work and knock up a meal almost instantly – a boon when you are tired and hungry after a long, hard day.

SERVES 2

250g (9oz) ready-made gnocchi

2 knobs of butter

125g (4½oz) freshly made pesto (*see* Ingredients note)

250g (9oz) gravadlax

olive oil, for brushing

sea salt and freshly ground black pepper

Cook the gnocchi in a saucepan of lightly salted boiling water according to the packet instructions until just tender. Drain and toss with the butter. Return the gnocchi to the cooking pan and stir in the pesto.

Heat the pan and cook the gnocchi in the pesto for about 2–3 minutes.

Season and keep warm.

Meanwhile, preheat the grill until hot. Lay the slices of gravadlax on the grill rack, brush lightly with oil and place under the hot grill for a few minutes until they turn light pink and just start to turn brown.

Tip the gnocchi into two warmed wide serving bowls and arrange the cooked gravadlax over the top. Grind over black pepper and serve.

Ingredients note Ideally buy freshly made pesto or make your own (*see* page 110), but otherwise a good rule of thumb is to look for pesto in a jar with the darkest colour you can find. This indicates that plenty of aromatic, fresh basil has been used.

vegetables

Potatoes and duck fat are a great combination and this is a dish after my own heart: I was brought up on bread and dripping, just as the French are brought up on goose or duck fat. Duck fat is sold like butter in France, but you can find it outside France in good delicatessens in cans and jars. Rosemary can be used instead of thyme.

Sautéed Potatoes with Garlic, Thyme and Duck Fat

SERVES 2

450g (1lb) new potatoes, scrubbed and dried

100ml (3½fl oz) duck fat

2 sprigs fresh thyme

½ whole garlic bulb

sea salt and freshly ground black pepper

Cut the potatoes in half and place in a heavy frying pan with the duck fat and fresh thyme.

Cut the garlic in half, skin and all. Add this to the pan, and cook the whole thing gently over a moderate heat for about 15–20 minutes until the potatoes are golden brown.

Season the potatoes with salt and pepper and serve them plus their fat in a bowl, alone, or with some French bread. For the health-conscious, drain off and save the flavoured duck fat for another use.

Crisp Potato Wedges with Mushy Peas and Balsamic Vinegar

This idea comes from my father. When I was younger and we lived on a farm, he used to eat three portions of fish and chips on his own, and finish with a chip butty with mushy peas and balsamic vinegar. As you can gather, he's not really into dieting! I've just taken the idea and turned it into a snack.

SERVES 2

oil, for deep-frying

1 x 600g can marrowfat peas, drained and rinsed

25g (1oz) butter

2 large baking potatoes, scrubbed

2 tbsp balsamic vinegar

sea salt and freshly ground black pepper

Preheat the oil in a deep pan or fryer to a high heat.

Tip the peas into another pan with the butter and a touch of water. Bring to the boil, and simmer gently for about 5 minutes until the peas go mushy. Remove from the heat.

Using a knife, not a peeler, cut the potatoes, skin and all, into smallish rough wedges. Place them, in batches, in the pan of oil and fry until golden brown. Remove and place on kitchen paper to get rid of excess oil.

Mix some seasoning and balsamic vinegar into the peas, to taste. Serve the potato wedges in a bowl with the peas on the side.

Tip Most supermarkets sell ready-cooked potato skins, which just need warming up in the oven: handy if you don't fancy deep-frying.

Chargrilled Vegetables with Olives and Goats' Cheese

A selection of ready-chargrilled vegetables packed in oil makes a wonderful basis for a quick starter or light main course, tossed with olives, dressed with pesto and topped with goats' cheese. Serve with hunks of country bread. Don't let the remainder of the oil drained from the vegetables go to waste. Use it to make dressings for salads or to drizzle over hot new potatoes.

SERVES 4

3–4 x 300g jars chargrilled vegetables in oil, e.g. artichokes, courgettes, aubergines, peppers and mushrooms, drained but the oil reserved

2 tbsp black olives

4 tbsp pesto

2 tbsp balsamic vinegar

2 tbsp chopped fresh herbs, e.g. oregano, dill, basil or parsley

2–3 tbsp toasted pinenuts

175g (6oz) goats' cheese

sea salt and freshly ground black pepper

Toss the chargrilled vegetables in a large bowl with the olives and seasoning, using plenty of pepper.

Mix the pesto with the vinegar and a little of the drained oil from the vegetables to taste. Add to the vegetables with the herbs and toss well. Divide between serving plates and scatter over the pinenuts.

Preheat the grill until hot. Slice the goats' cheese into 4 rounds and grill on one side until bubbling, golden brown and soft in the centre. Lift from the grill rack using a palette knife and place on top of the vegetables. Serve immediately.

Ingredients note I use Spanish ingredients for this dish – olives from Aragon and montenebro cheese.

A simple early summer feast, ideal as a starter. I look forward to May when a local farmer from the Hampshire village of Chabolton supplies me with bundles of his superb green asparagus spears. He was one of my suppliers at the Hotel du Vin in Winchester, and would happily pick spears to order.

Griddled Asparagus with Roasted Red Peppers

SERVES 4

2 bunches of green asparagus, about 500g (1lb 2oz)

2 large red peppers, halved lengthways and deseeded

olive oil, for brushing

50g (1¾oz) unsalted butter, melted

sea salt and freshly ground black pepper

To prepare the asparagus spears, trim the bases and use a swivel vegetable peeler to shave the woody stems. Bring a large pan of salted water to the boil and have a large bowl of iced cold water at the ready.

Blanch the asparagus for 2–3 minutes in the boiling water, then drain and immediately drop into the bowl of iced water. This prevents any further cooking and maintains the colour.

While the asparagus is cooling, preheat the oven to 200°C/400°F/gas mark 6. Place the peppers, cut side down, on a baking sheet and brush the skins with oil.

Roast the peppers in the oven for about 15 minutes or until the skins blacken and blister. Remove to a bowl and cover with clingfilm. Leave for 5 minutes, then peel off the skins.

Heat a griddle pan until you can feel a good heat rising. Place the asparagus spears on to the hot metal and allow to char slightly. Transfer to warmed serving plates and arrange in a spray pattern. Season well. Position the pepper halves at the base of the spears and drizzle over the melted butter.

This is a dish I made for *Ready Steady Cook* on television. A batter for deep-frying can be made in a number of ways – plain, with yeast or with baking powder – but using beer gives good flavour and makes the batter crisp up very well. This batter can also be used to deep-fry fish, fruit or other vegetables, such as carrot, courgette and aubergine. You could even combine a selection of vegetable fritters to serve with this or any other relevant dip. Try other mayonnaise flavours as well, such as rocket and lemon.

Red Pepper Fritters with Garlic Mayonnaise

SERVES 2

2 red peppers

oil, for deep-frying

sea salt and freshly ground black pepper

BATTER

150g (5½oz) self-raising flour

250ml (9fl oz) good bitter or ale

15g (½oz) fresh coriander, chopped

GARLIC MAYONNAISE

200ml (7fl oz) mayonnaise

1 tbsp garlic purée

Cut the peppers in half, remove the seeds and stalks and slice them into 2cm (¾in) strips.

Heat the oil in a deep-fryer or deep pan to a high heat.

To make the batter, place the flour in a bowl, season well and slowly add the beer, mixing well with a whisk. Add the chopped coriander. The batter should be thick and glutinous.

Dip the pepper strips in the batter, let any excess drip away and deep-fry in batches until golden brown. Remove and place on kitchen paper to drain, then season with a little salt.

Mix the mayonnaise with the garlic purée and place in a bowl on a platter. Arrange the fritters around the bowl. Eat them just warm, dipped in the mayonnaise.

Hot Waffles with Sun-dried Tomatoes and Minted Cream

Waffles should be bought fresh, not frozen, as the frozen ones tend to break and crumble when cooking, however carefully they've been thawed out. Good fresh ones are moist and require less butter, which makes them a little healthier. This dish is very quick to make – about 10 minutes. It is also good as a quick lunch snack. But the waffles need to be served warm for the dish to work.

SERVES 2

2 fresh waffles, about 35g (1¼oz) each

85g (3oz) crème fraîche

1 tbsp chopped fresh mint, plus extra to garnish

60g (2¼oz) butter, melted

6 sun-dried tomatoes in oil

Place the waffles under a preheated hot grill to colour both sides: a few minutes only.

Mix the crème fraîche and chopped mint together and leave to one side.

Remove the waffles from the grill, brush well with the melted butter and put on the plates. Spoon the minted crème fraîche on top, garnish with the sun-dried tomatoes and mint leaves, then serve.

Bubble and Squeak Cakes

I love a fry-up, and this is simply a more elegant way of serving the classic, ever-popular 'bubble and squeak'.

MAKES 4

500g (1lb 2oz) floury potatoes, e.g. king edward, maris piper or desirée, chopped

125g (4½oz) green cabbage, shredded

olive or sunflower oil, for frying

3 rashers smoked bacon, rinded and chopped

1 shallot, peeled and chopped

2 garlic cloves, peeled and crushed

3 tbsp chopped mixed fresh herbs, e.g. parsley, dill or coriander

seasoned flour, for coating

sea salt and freshly ground black pepper

Boil the potatoes in lightly salted water for about 15 minutes until just tender, then drain well and mash in the pan. Leave in the pan.

Blanch the cabbage in a little boiling water for 2 minutes, then drain, rinse under cold running water and pat dry with kitchen paper.

Heat a trickle of oil in a frying pan, add the bacon and fry until crisp. Remove and drain on kitchen paper. Add 1 tbsp oil to the pan, add the shallot and garlic and sauté for 3 minutes until softened.

Add the shallot and garlic to the mashed potato with the cabbage, bacon, chopped herbs and seasoning. Set aside to cool.

Shape the mixture into 4 cakes. Toss in seasoned flour to coat, shaking off any excess. Heat oil to a depth of 1cm (½in) in a large frying pan. Lower the cakes into the hot oil using a fish slice and cook for about 3 minutes on each side, turning them carefully. Remove and drain on kitchen paper. Serve immediately.

Serving note These delicious cakes can be served with all sorts of dishes, from the sophisticated Pepper-crusted Monkfish with Mustard Dill Sauce (*see* page 66), to a humble plate of eggs and bacon.

Baba Ganoush

This aubergine purée, made with tahina, a sesame seed paste, is ideal cold as a dip, or served hot as a garnish for lamb. Chefs who go in for fancy recipe titles call this 'aubergine caviar'. I much prefer its original Arabic name, which apparently means 'spoilt old man'. Mint and lemon are the predominant flavours here, but coriander and lime could be used for a change.

SERVES 4

2 large aubergines

olive oil, for frying

2 tbsp light tahina

3 garlic cloves, peeled and chopped

10 walnut halves

juice and grated zest of 1 lemon

15g (½oz) fresh mint

sea salt and freshly ground black pepper

Cut the aubergines in half lengthways. Cut slits into the flesh in a zig-zag fashion, but do not pierce the skin.

In a hot pan, cook the aubergines in 1cm (½in) olive oil, flesh side down first, for about 2 minutes. Then turn over and cook on the other side until soft and tender.

Place the aubergine flesh and skin, plus the tahina, garlic, walnuts, lemon and mint, into a food processor or blender. Purée until smooth.

Season well, and serve with a salad or with breadsticks.

Serving note Lightly warmed through, the Baba Ganoush is wonderful served with charred or seared salmon. It's also good served cold with cold cooked salmon.

Crème fraîche makes a really good dressing, especially for smothering over sliced buffalo mozzarella. Use half-fat crème fraîche for a lighter sauce. The red onion and spinach add colour as well as flavour.

Marinated Mozzarella with Red Onion and Spinach

SERVES 4

4 balls of buffalo mozzarella cheese, about 100g (3½oz) each

200g (7oz) crème fraîche (full or half fat)

2–3 tbsp extra virgin olive oil

1 garlic clove, peeled and chopped

2 tbsp chopped fresh herbs, e.g. parsley, basil, oregano or dill

1 tbsp balsamic vinegar

200g (7oz) baby leaf spinach

½ red onion, peeled and thinly sliced

sea salt and freshly ground black pepper

Drain the mozzarella balls of milk (reserving the milk if using full-fat crème fraîche – see below), then cut each into 4–5 slices.

Whisk the crème fraîche with 1 tbsp of the oil, the garlic, half the chopped herbs and seasoning. (If using full-fat crème fraîche, you may want to thin the dressing down a little with some of the mozzarella milk.)

Toss the mozzarella slices with the crème fraîche dressing and chill in the refrigerator for about 1 hour.

Meanwhile, whisk together the remaining oil, the vinegar and seasoning. When ready to serve, toss the spinach with the onion in the vinegar dressing, then divide between four serving plates. Spoon the dressed cheese on top, season with pepper and scatter over the remaining herbs.

Aubergine and Mozzarella Stacks

This is the sort of dish you could pay serious money for in a restaurant, but is in fact quite easy to put together. You bake sliced aubergines and buffalo mozzarella in layers, sprinkled in between with a classic Italian gremolata – a blend of parsley, garlic and lemon. Serve with a homemade spicy tomato sauce, but if time is short, a good ready-made tomato sauce rich in oil and garlic will stand in for the homemade version.

SERVES 4

2 large aubergines, sliced 1cm (½in) thick

olive oil, for brushing

1 mugful of fresh flat-leaf parsley

3 garlic cloves, peeled and finely chopped

grated zest of 1 lemon

1 tsp chopped fresh rosemary

4 balls of buffalo mozzarella cheese, about 100g (3½oz) each

sea salt and freshly ground black pepper

SAUCE

1 tbsp olive oil

1 shallot, peeled and finely chopped

1 small plump red chilli, deseeded and chopped

1 garlic clove, peeled and finely chopped

8 ripe plum tomatoes, skinned and chopped

a good pinch of sugar

2 tbsp chopped fresh basil

Preheat the oven to 180°C/350°F/gas mark 4.

Brush the aubergine slices with oil and season lightly. Heat a ridged griddle pan until you feel a good heat rising. Add the aubergine slices and chargrill for about 3 minutes on each side until softened. You need to do this in batches. Remove and leave to cool.

To make the gremolata, finely chop the parsley sprigs and mix with the garlic, lemon zest and rosemary.

Cut the balls of mozzarella into 1cm (½in) slices. Divide the mozzarella and aubergine slices into 4 equal portions. Layer the slices alternately on a lightly greased baking sheet, sprinkling the gremolata and seasoning between each layer, to make 4 stacks, using the larger pieces for the bases and the smaller pieces on top.

Bake the stacks in the oven for about 15 minutes until the cheese just starts to melt.

Meanwhile, to make the sauce, heat the oil in a frying pan, add the shallot, chilli and garlic and sauté for about 5 minutes. Add the chopped tomatoes, sugar and seasoning. Cook for about 10 minutes, stirring occasionally, until you have a thick sauce. Add the basil, then leave to cool. Transfer to a food processor or blender and process to make a purée. Reheat the sauce in a clean saucepan and keep warm.

Place each stack in the centre of a warmed serving plate with the sauce spooned alongside.

Celeriac Remoulade

This is a popular salad in France, and is sometimes sold here packed in small plastic pots. However, the homemade version is far nicer. You can serve celeriac raw, although some people prefer it blanched in boiling water for 1 minute. The sauce is a mustard mayonnaise livened up with my special touches. You can either make your own mayonnaise or use a good-quality ready-made one, such as the French brand Delouis Fils.

SERVES 4

500g (1lb 2oz) celeriac

1 red onion, peeled and thinly sliced

250ml (9fl oz) thick mayonnaise

3 tbsp coarse-grain mustard, e.g. Pommery or Gordons

juice and grated zest of 1 lemon

a dash of Worcestershire sauce

1–2 tbsp milk (optional)

2 tbsp chopped fresh parsley

sea salt and freshly ground black pepper

Peel the celeriac, then slice it as thinly as possible (use a mandoline if you have one). Stack the slices 3 or 4 at a time on top of each other and cut into long, thin julienne or matchsticks.

Place in a bowl and mix with the onion. (If you prefer a milder flavour, first soak the onion in a large bowl of cold water for 1 hour.)

Beat the mayonnaise with the mustard, lemon zest and juice, Worcestershire sauce and seasoning. Combine with the celeriac and onion. If you find the sauce a little too thick, thin it with a little milk. Check the seasoning, stir in the parsley and serve in an attractive bowl.

This may sound an unlikely combination of flavours, but, trust me, it's delicious. Celeriac is a large, knobbly skinned, turnip-like vegetable, which is quite often sold in the major supermarkets and upmarket greengrocers. Beneath its unattractive, pock-marked skin lies firm flesh with a fine, fennel-like flavour.

Roast Celeriac with Vanilla and Garlic

SERVES 4

1kg (2lb 4oz) celeriac

1 bourbon vanilla pod (*see* Ingredients note, page 259)

50g (1¾oz) butter, softened

4 tbsp olive oil

3 garlic cloves, unpeeled and crushed

sea salt and freshly ground black pepper

Preheat the oven to 180°C/350°F/gas mark 4.

Peel the celeriac – you may find this easier to do if you first cut the vegetable into large chunks. Once they are peeled, cut the large chunks into smaller ones.

Slit the vanilla pod lengthways and with the tip of a knife scrape out the tiny seeds into the butter. Blend well.

Place the celeriac in a roasting pan, drizzle with the oil and dot with the vanilla-flavoured butter. Season well. Scatter around the crushed garlic cloves and add the empty vanilla pod.

Roast in the oven for about 40 minutes, stirring once or twice, until softened. Spoon into a warmed serving dish to serve.

Serving note This celeriac dish makes an ideal accompaniment for roasted meat or grilled fish.

Caramelized Beetroot

A speedy, simple serving idea for cooked beetroot. You can use ready-cooked beets from a pack but be sure to avoid the variety contained in that awful vinegar. But better still, cook and peel your own fresh beetroot.

SERVES 4

3 tbsp clear honey

25g (1oz) butter

4 whole cooked beetroots, cut in half

juice of 1 lemon

1 tbsp chopped fresh parsley

sea salt and freshly ground black pepper

Heat a large non-stick frying pan until you feel a good heat rising. Spoon in the honey and swirl in the butter.

When you have a golden-brown glaze, add the beetroot halves with the lemon juice and cook for 3–5 minutes, spooning the honey juices constantly over the beetroot.

Season well and tip into a warmed serving dish. Scatter over the parsley and serve.

Serving note This dish is great served with roast lamb, chicken or pork.

Deep-fried Parsnip Chips

This snack, ideal with a drink, is very simple to make. You can use other vegetables instead of or as well as the parsnips, such as carrots, beetroots, courgettes and, of course, potatoes. A mixture in a bowl looks and tastes great. The chips can also be used to garnish main-course dishes too, as can deep-fried herbs which are also tasty as a finger food, especially when sprinkled with salt and toasted sesame seeds.

SERVES 2

2 large firm parsnips, scrubbed

oil, for deep-frying

sea salt

Put the oil in a deep pan or fryer, and heat until very hot. If possible, use a metal basket as it makes it easier to move the chips around and lift them out of the oil.

Using a potato peeler, peel long strips of parsnip, skin and all, down the length of the vegetables.

Carefully place a handful of the parsnip strips in the oil and keep moving the basket to stop them sticking. When the parsnips are a light golden colour, not brown, remove and drain on kitchen paper.

Season with a little salt, and keep warm while you deep-fry the remaining parsnip chips.

Chilli Garlic-dressed Mushrooms

This is a wow of a dish, which can be served as a starter or, if smaller mushrooms are used, for tapas. Make sure you use a good-quality olive oil.

SERVES 4

8–12 field mushrooms, depending on size

100ml (3½fl oz) extra virgin olive oil

2 fat garlic cloves, peeled and chopped

½ large red chilli, deseeded and chopped

1 shallot, peeled and chopped

1 tbsp lemon juice

sea salt and freshly ground black pepper

Preheat the grill until hot. Wipe the mushrooms clean, if necessary (do not wash them – it makes them slimy). Brush the tops and gills with about half the oil and season. Grill for about 3 minutes on each side until softened.

Meanwhile, whisk the remaining oil with the garlic, chilli, shallot, lemon juice and seasoning.

Place the mushrooms in a shallow serving dish, pour over the dressing and mix thoroughly. Leave until cooled to room temperature before serving.

Serving note These mushrooms are lovely served with crusty bread to mop up the juices.

Variation You could make this dish with large button mushrooms in place of field mushrooms. Pan-fry in olive oil instead of grilling them.

Butter Bean and Rosemary Purée

There was a period in the 1980s when vegetables were often served as a purée. Like all fashions, it eventually lost its appeal and purées became *passé*. Despite this, I like to serve meats and fish nestling on a small bed of purée. Not only does them to the plate – an attribute greatly appreciated by enthusiastic waiters – and it also adds a creamy contrast to the rest of the dish. This particular recipe is another popular idea from my days working at the 190 restaurant in Queen's Gate in South Kensington, London, with my mentor, Anthony Worrall Thompson. Use Spanish butter beans; otherwise French haricots would be a good alternative. You can make the purée in advance and simply reheat it before serving.

SERVES 4

175g (6oz) dried white beans (*see* recipe introduction)

1 tbsp olive oil

3 shallots, peeled and chopped

3 fat garlic cloves, peeled and crushed

3 rashers smoked bacon or pancetta, rinded and chopped

leaves stripped from 1 sprig fresh rosemary, chopped

1 sprig fresh thyme

150ml (¼ pint) dry white wine

400ml (14fl oz) fresh chicken or vegetable stock

2–4 tbsp double cream or crème fraîche

sea salt and freshly ground black pepper

Soak the beans in water overnight, then drain and rinse. Place in a saucepan, cover with cold water and bring to the boil. Continue to boil for 5 minutes, then drain.

Meanwhile, heat the oil in a frying pan, add the shallots, garlic and bacon or pancetta and sauté for 5 minutes. Add the blanched beans with the rosemary, thyme, wine and stock. Bring to the boil, then season with pepper only.

Cover and simmer for about 30 minutes until the beans are softened. Remove the lid, add salt to season and boil again to evaporate any remaining liquid. Remove the thyme sprig and transfer the bean mixture to a food processor or blender. Add the cream or crème fraîche and whizz to a purée. Serve hot.

Variation You can make a quicker version of this dish using 2 x 400g cans butter beans in place of the dried butter beans. Simply drain and rinse the beans, then add them to the sautéed shallots, garlic and bacon or pancetta with the herbs and wine, but without the stock. Simmer for 15 minutes, then blend with the cream or crème fraîche to make a purée.

soups

Bread is used throughout Continental Europe to thicken soups, whereas people in Britain tend to use flour or potato. I've used two types of tomato here: the fresh tomatoes to give texture and canned tomatoes to give colour and flavour. Please don't try to purée this soup when it's ready. It's meant to be rustic in look and texture – good wholesome food. This is a very easy soup: the whole thing can be made from start to finish in about five minutes.

Rustic Tomato, Bread and Basil Soup

SERVES 4

about 3 tbsp olive oil, plus extra for drizzling

1 red onion, peeled and diced

6 garlic cloves, peeled and diced

300ml (½ pint) white wine

150ml (¼ pint) water

12 plum tomatoes, quartered

2 x 400g cans plum tomatoes

½ loaf ciabatta

15g (½oz) fresh basil

sea salt and freshly ground black pepper

Heat the olive oil in a pan, and cook the onion and garlic for a few minutes to soften them slightly.

Add the wine, water and all the tomatoes. Cover with a lid, bring to the boil and season with salt and lots of pepper.

Dice the bread and stir it into the soup, along with the freshly ripped basil leaves. Place in soup bowls, drizzle with olive oil on the top and serve.

You don't need to worry about using dried butter beans for this soup, as the canned ones are perfect. The soup is good enough just made with beans and finished off with truffle oil, but the addition of the chorizo gives it an extra spicy kick.

Chorizo, Butter Bean and Truffle Oil Soup

SERVES 4

1 very small chorizo sausage, sliced

½ small onion, peeled and chopped

2 garlic cloves, peeled and chopped

1 tbsp olive oil

2 x 400g cans butter beans

200ml (7fl oz) white wine

500ml (18fl oz) fresh chicken stock

2 sprigs each fresh thyme and parsley

200ml (7fl oz) double cream

truffle oil (*see* Tip, page 159)

sea salt and freshly ground black pepper

Place the chorizo, onion and garlic into a hot pan with the oil and sauté slowly for a few minutes until the chorizo softens slightly.

Drain the beans, rinse and drain again, then add to the pan with the wine and stock. Bring to the boil, add the thyme and parsley, and simmer for about 10 minutes.

Using a blender, purée the soup until all the lumps have gone.

Add the cream and seasoning, heat through a little, then place in soup bowls. Finish with a drizzle of truffle oil. Serve with some chunky pieces of bread.

This was a dish created on the BBC's *Food and Drink* programme for a blind-date dance for 350 Durham University students. It had to be an aphrodisiac meal, so I included some oysters. As these are very expensive, they're only optional. If using, remove from the shells, poach in a little champagne for two minutes, then serve floating on top of the soup. Celeriac is an under-used vegetable, although it's delicious and versatile. It can be puréed like potato, or puréed with potato; it's great flavoured with a vanilla pod and some curry powder; and it can also be blanched in small chips and served as a remoulade salad – thin slices with mustard and mayonnaise, *see* page 146 – as a starter.

Cream of Celeriac Soup with Truffle Oil

SERVES 4

1 medium celeriac, chopped

¼ leek, chopped

½ carrot, chopped

½ white onion, peeled and chopped

2 garlic cloves, peeled and chopped

25g (1oz) butter

100ml (3½fl oz) white wine

l litre (1¾ pints) fresh chicken stock

200ml (7fl oz) double cream

truffle oil (*see* Tip)

oysters and champagne, for poaching (optional)

sea salt and freshly ground black pepper

Prepare the vegetables first, just before cooking. Remember that the smaller you cut them, the quicker the soup will be made. (If you want to do the preparation in advance, put the celeriac in water with a little lemon juice; otherwise it will turn brown.)

Put the butter, onion and garlic in a hot pan and cook for a few minutes, then add the celeriac, leek, carrot, white wine and stock. Bring to the boil and cook until the vegetables are soft: about 10–20 minutes.

Purée the vegetables and liquid with the cream in a food processor or blender until smooth. Season well and place in bowls. To finish, drizzle with a little truffle oil, before serving.

Tip Get someone rich to buy you some truffle oil. The best comes in a small square bottle and is very expensive, but it is extremely potent (with a much more concentrated flavour than others). Just a trickle on this soup – or on a dish of pasta – is unequalled. To make truffle oil go a little further, mix it with some olive oil (not extra virgin): 100ml (3½fl oz) truffle oil mixed with 400ml (14fl oz) olive oil gives an oil that is still bursting with flavour.

Thai Prawn and Noodle Soup

Classic Thai soups often consist of clear broth poured into bowls, piled high with thin rice vermicelli noodles. This is a quick adaptation of a salmon and lobster soup that I occasionally make. Here I've used fresh tiger prawns and added the shells to bought fresh fish stock to enrich its flavour and colour.

SERVES 4

300g (10½oz) whole uncooked tiger prawns, thawed if frozen

1 tsp coriander seeds

2cm (¾in) piece fresh galangal or 1cm (½in) piece fresh root ginger, sliced (*see* Ingredients note)

800ml (1 pint 7fl oz) fresh fish stock

200g (7oz) thin rice or egg noodles (*see* Ingredients note)

3 tbsp Thai fish sauce

2 fat red chillies, deseeded and thinly sliced

2–4 garlic cloves (to taste), peeled and thinly sliced

1 salmon fillet, about 200g (7oz), skinned and cut into small cubes

4 spring onions, chopped

1 tbsp chopped fresh coriander

1 tbsp chopped fresh mint

juice of 1 lemon or 2 limes

a little sesame oil (optional)

sea salt and freshly ground black pepper

Peel and despine the prawns (as shown below), reserve the shells and set aside. Place the prawn shells, coriander seeds and galangal or ginger in a saucepan with the stock. Bring to the boil, then simmer gently for 5 minutes. Leave to stand for 10 minutes before straining. Return the strained stock to the pan.

Meanwhile, reconstitute the noodles according to the packet instructions. Drain and keep warm.

Bring the stock back to the boil and add the fish sauce, chillies and garlic. Reduce the heat and simmer for 2 minutes. Add the prawns to the pan with the salmon, and return to a simmer to cook gently for about 3 minutes, until both are firm and cooked. Add the onions, herbs and lemon or lime juice to taste.

Divide the noodles between soup bowls. Using a slotted spoon, lift out the prawns, fish and flavourings and place around the noodles. Season the hot stock and pour into the bowls. Drizzle over a little sesame oil, if desired, before serving.

Ingredients note Galangal is available in most Asian food stores – it is similar to fresh root ginger, but milder. You can also buy the noodles from Asian food stores, although many supermarkets sell a good selection.

salads & antipasti

Warm Salad of New Potatoes, Raclette Cheese and Red Pepper

Whenever you have any left-over new potatoes, this is what you could do instead of simply frying them in butter: make a meal of them. This is great as a starter with a glass of chardonnay, but could make a filling lunch dish as well. Here I suggest bought tapenade made with olives, but if you don't like olives (like me), use Sun-dried Tomato Tapenade (see page 179).

SERVES 4

1 red pepper

6 tbsp olive oil, plus extra for drizzling

3 tbsp balsamic vinegar

225g (8oz) cooked new potatoes

3 tbsp grain mustard

1 sprig fresh rosemary, chopped

85g (3oz) raclette (or Gruyère) cheese, grated

½ head frisée lettuce

60g (2¼oz) tapenade

4 sprigs fresh basil

sea salt and freshly ground black pepper

Preheat the oven to 200°C/400°F/gas mark 6.

Cut the red pepper in half, discard the seeds and stalk, and place, cut side down, on an oven tray. Drizzle with olive oil and bake in the oven until the skin is brown, about 15–20 minutes. Remove from the oven, place in a bowl, cover with clingfilm while hot and leave to cool. Peel the skin off the pepper and cut the flesh into small dice.

Mix the pepper dice with the olive oil, the vinegar and some seasoning to make the dressing.

Dice the cooked potatoes, skin and all, and put in a bowl with the mustard, seasoning and the chopped fresh rosemary. Place in a microwave for about 30 seconds to warm up and then press into four 5cm (2in) stainless-steel rings on a baking tray. Top with the grated cheese. (At this stage, if you haven't got a microwave, put into the still-warm oven, or a low oven, to soften the cheese and heat the potatoes through.) Place under a preheated hot grill to brown the top.

Place a small pile of frisée leaves in the middle of each plate and sit the ring of potato and cheese on the top. Lift the steel ring off, leaving the moulded shape on the leaves, cheese on the top. Spoon a mound of the tapenade on top of the cheese or serve it in a small bowl on the side.

Chop the fresh basil and add to the red pepper dressing. Check for seasoning again. Spoon round the edges of the plates and serve.

Come May and June, baby new potatoes are at their best – full of flavour with a smooth, velvety texture. My favourite are the kidney-shaped Jersey Royals, but other parts of Britain produce excellent new spuds too – Cornwall, Pembroke, Kent and Scotland. This recipe originates from my days at the Chewton Glen Hotel in Hampshire, and is a good salad to serve as a starter. It can also be turned into a special side dish for a buffet party. The dressing is a simple blend of cream, lemon and truffle oil. Buy the best concentrated oil you can afford – it will repay you in a greater depth of flavour. But if you are really pushing the boat out, treat yourself to an actual truffle. You can buy small black ones and eke them out by slicing wafer thin on a mandoline or even a special truffle shaver. The fragrance of a fresh truffle is a waft of paradise.

New Potato Salad with Truffle Cream Dressing

SERVES 4

500g (1lb 2oz) small new potatoes, scrubbed

½ frisée lettuce

125ml (4fl oz) double cream

juice of 1 small lemon

1 tbsp truffle oil

2 tbsp extra virgin olive oil

1 tbsp balsamic vinegar

1 tbsp chopped fresh chives

shavings from ½ small black truffle (optional but well worth trying)

sea salt and freshly ground black pepper

Boil the potatoes in their skins in a saucepan of lightly salted water for about 15 minutes until tender but not overcooked. Drain well and leave to cool a little. When cool enough to handle, peel, then cut into 1cm (½in) slices. Season well and set aside.

Pick over the frisée, discarding any discoloured or damaged leaves, and tear into bite-sized pieces. Place in a bowl.

Whip the cream until frothy, then beat in the lemon juice (or as much as it takes to sour the cream), seasoning and the truffle oil.

Whisk the olive oil with the balsamic vinegar and seasoning, add to the frisée and toss well. Divide between four serving plates.

Mix the potatoes gently with the cream dressing and pile on top of the frisée. Sprinkle over the chives and season again. Scatter over the truffle slices (if using), and serve.

Green-pea Guacamole with Nachos

Frozen peas have a superb flavour and require very little cooking. Here they are not cooked at all, just defrosted to make a quick dip or spread. This recipe can also serve as a salsa, and is particularly good with grilled or barbecued merguez, the hot, spicy, thin sausages from Algeria, which are available from delicatessens, good butchers and some supermarkets. Be careful when cooking them as they smoke a lot because of the amount of fat they contain. If you don't like dips that are too spicy, leave out the chilli, but do keep the cumin – using a little more perhaps – as this complements the flavour of the peas.

SERVES 4

450g (1lb) frozen peas

½ small red onion, peeled and finely chopped

1 garlic clove, peeled and finely chopped

10 fresh mint leaves

115g (4oz) plain yoghurt

½ red chilli, deseeded and finely chopped

1 tsp ground cumin

olive oil, for drizzling

nachos, to serve

sea salt and freshly ground black pepper

Defrost the peas and thoroughly drain off any water.

Place the peas in a food processor together with the onion, garlic and mint and purée slightly. Add the yoghurt and purée again.

Remove from the processor and stir in the chilli and ground cumin. Add salt and pepper to taste.

Place in a bowl, drizzle some olive oil on the top and dig in with the nachos.

Tip If you do not have a food processor at home, use a hand-operated vegetable mill, or a mortar and pestle. Alternatively, you can crush the peas with a potato masher before mixing with everything else: this makes for a much coarser texture.

Grilled Goats' Cheese with a Broad Bean, Pancetta and Mint Salad

A dish that can be rustled up in a couple of minutes from just a few supermarket ingredients, which looks and tastes sensational. Pancetta is an Italian cured and rolled belly pork, which is much tastier than the British type of bacon. It contains plenty of fat, so is ideal for cooking with other ingredients. Don't add any extra fat to the pan as it is the fat being rendered – the fat coming out of the pancetta – that crisps the meat. You can buy pancetta in Italian delicatessens or diced in many supermarkets.

SERVES 2

2 slices Italian white bread (ciabatta or focaccia)

olive oil, for drizzling

125g (4½oz) pancetta, diced

1 garlic clove, peeled and diced

¼ red onion, peeled and diced

3 tbsp balsamic vinegar

1 x 100g (3½oz) piece goats' cheese (*see* Tip), cut in half

225g (8oz) frozen broad beans, defrosted and peeled (*see* Tip)

1 tbsp pesto

2 tbsp chopped fresh mint

30g (½oz) fresh basil

rock salt and freshly ground black pepper

Preheat the oven to 200°C/400°F/gas mark 6.

Place the slices of bread on an ovenproof tray, drizzle with olive oil, sprinkle with rock salt and bake in the oven for about 5 minutes until crisp but not coloured.

In a hot pan, cook the pancetta without any added fat until crisp and golden brown. Then add the diced garlic, onion and vinegar, and cook together for 1 minute. Remove from the heat.

Preheat the grill. Put the goats' cheese on the bread, season with salt and pepper, and drizzle with olive oil. Place under the grill until golden brown.

Add the peeled beans, pesto and mint to the bacon mix. Stir well and season to taste. Place the bean mix on two plates, top with the goats' cheese and bread, drizzle with olive oil and garnish with sprigs of fresh basil.

Ingredients note Goats' cheese has a sharp taste that goes well with broad beans. Try to get a young Sainte-Maure or Crottin de Chavignol, or a British Gedi. More mature goats' cheeses tend to be crumbly and have a concentrated chalky flavour which some people find off-putting.

Tip To reveal the attractive bright green interior of broad beans (frozen or fresh) blanch them in boiling water for about 30 seconds, then drain. Cover with cold water to stop the cooking and drain again. Peel off the outer skin. This dish definitely works better with frozen beans than with fresh.

When ripe sweet black figs are in season, serve them as a chic hot starter stuffed with nuggets of blue cheese and wrapped in Italian prosciutto. They take next to no time to prepare and only a few minutes to cook.

Figs Roasted with Blue Cheese and Prosciutto

SERVES 4

8 ripe black figs

250g (9oz) soft blue cheese, e.g. Roquefort, Pipo Crème, Dolcelatte or blue Brie

8 thin slices prosciutto

olive oil, for brushing

2 tbsp balsamic vinegar

2 tbsp chopped fresh mint

freshly ground black pepper

Cut the figs almost in half from top to bottom but leaving the halves attached at the base. Open out the 2 halves.

Cut the blue cheese into 8 cubes and sandwich between the fig halves. Close up the fig halves.

Lay the prosciutto slices flat on a board. Place one stuffed fig on each slice and roll up. Place on a baking sheet and brush lightly with the oil. When nearly ready to serve, preheat the oven to 190°C/375°F/gas mark 5.

Drizzle the vinegar over the figs and bake in the oven for 8–10 minutes until the prosciutto crisps up and before the cheese starts to ooze out of the figs. Serve immediately, with any pan juices spooned over and sprinkled with chopped mint and freshly ground black pepper.

Bresaola is air-cured beef from Italy, served in much the same way as Parma ham – that is, wafer thin with one or two simple accompaniments. One of the garnishes I like to serve with it is pieces of lemon zest cooked in sugar syrup. It may sound odd, but it's a winning combination. If you have a swivel vegetable peeler and half an hour to spare, you can make up a batch to store in the refrigerator, ready to serve when you want to impress your dinner guests. Any unused pieces of zest can be stored in the syrup in a jam jar.

Bresaola with Confit Lemon Rind and Rocket Salad

SERVES 4

4 unwaxed lemons

85g (3oz) caster sugar

300ml (½ pint) water

200g (7oz) wild rocket leaves

3–4 tbsp extra virgin olive oil

200g (7oz) bresaola, sliced wafer thin

50g (1¾oz) Parmesan

sea salt and freshly ground black pepper

Peel the zest from the lemons using a swivel vegetable peeler, making sure that you don't include any of the white pith. If the strips of zest are long, cut them into lengths of about 2cm (¾in).

Place the sugar and water in a saucepan and heat gently until the sugar is dissolved. Bring to the boil, stirring. Drop in the pieces of zest and simmer for about 15 minutes until they become translucent. Leave to cool in the syrup, then drain well and pat dry with kitchen paper.

Season the rocket leaves, then dress with the oil.

Lay out the bresaola slices on four serving plates, spreading them thinly. Place an equal portion of the rocket salad in the centre of each plate. Sprinkle over as many pieces of zest as you like.

Shave the Parmesan into wafer-thin slices and scatter over the plates. Grind over pepper and serve.

Salad of Roasted Peppers and Olives

This dish goes well with a simple grill of steaks or fish. Alternatively, serve as part of tapas with Brandade of Salt Cod (see page 60).

SERVES 4

2 large red peppers, halved lengthways and deseeded

2–3 tbsp good-quality, aged balsamic vinegar

1 tbsp chopped fresh oregano or marjoram, or 1 tsp dried

1 shallot, peeled and finely chopped

a small handful of black olives, pitted and roughly chopped

sea salt and whole black peppercorns, to taste

Preheat the oven to 200°C/400°F/gas mark 6. Place the peppers, cut side down, on a baking sheet. Roast for 15–20 minutes until the skins start to char. Remove from the baking sheet, place in a bowl while still hot, cover with clingfilm and allow to cool. Peel off the skins – they should be fairly easy to remove, but it doesn't matter if a little remains.

Cut the peppers into strips and place in a serving bowl. Crack the whole black peppercorns with the flat side of a wide-blade knife or a rolling pin. Drizzle the vinegar over the peppers and stir in the herb, shallot, olives, salt and cracked peppercorns. Allow to cool before serving.

Serving note This salad is also good served with poppy seed grissini, which you can make by simply rolling breadsticks in crème fraîche, then tossing in poppy seeds. Eat them quite quickly, before they go soggy.

Roasted Peppers Marinated in Balsamic Vinegar and Herbs

Try this piled on to some charred bread, or just eaten on its own with a fork as part of an antipasto. If cut into chunks instead of strips, the peppers make a good garnish for hot cooked salmon, charred smoked salmon or cold chicken. If you decant the peppers into jam jars, they make a great present. Packets of Italian herbs usually contain the soft herbs oregano, basil, tarragon and flat-leaf parsley.

SERVES 2

1 red pepper

1 green pepper

1 yellow pepper

50ml (2fl oz) olive oil, plus extra for drizzling

¼ red onion, peeled and finely diced

2 garlic cloves, peeled and finely diced

75ml (2½fl oz) balsamic vinegar

30g (½oz) Italian herbs, chopped

sea salt and freshly ground black pepper

Preheat the oven to 220°C/425°F/gas mark 7.

Halve the peppers, remove the seeds and stalks, and place the halves on an ovenproof tray. Drizzle with olive oil and place in the oven until the skin is well coloured: about 15–20 minutes. Remove from the oven, and while the peppers are still hot, put them in a bowl and cover with clingfilm.

Mix the onion and garlic with the olive oil, the vinegar and chopped Italian herbs. Season with salt and pepper and leave to one side.

When the peppers are cool, peel off the skins and cut the flesh into 2cm (¾in) strips. Pour in the marinade and season well. Eat straight away or keep in the fridge for up to 24 hours.

Tip Using clingfilm to cover the bowl of peppers traps any steam, which encourages the skin to rise up off the flesh. This is much quicker and less messy than burning the skins off over a naked flame.

If you don't have enough time to roast the peppers yourself, buy 2 x 400g cans or jars of roasted red peppers.

Salad of Two Smoked Fish

There are some excellent small local smokehouses now selling an impressive range of smoked fish. This quick salad features smoked trout and eel with a creamy horseradish sauce, in perfect contrast to crisp bacon and bitter salad leaves. It is substantial enough to serve as a light meal.

SERVES 4

100ml (3½fl oz) fresh fish stock

2 tbsp horseradish sauce

225g (8oz) smoked streaky bacon rashers, rinded

300g (10½oz) smoked trout fillets

300g (10½z) smoked eel fillets

100ml (3½fl oz) double cream

about 200g (7oz) frisée lettuce or other bitter frilly leaves, torn into pieces

4 tbsp chopped fresh parsley

2 tbsp chopped fresh chives

extra virgin olive oil, for drizzling

sea salt and freshly ground black pepper

Heat the stock in a saucepan until boiling and continue to boil, uncovered, until reduced by half. Leave to cool a little. Place the horseradish sauce in a bowl and beat in the reduced stock to form a purée. Set aside to cool.

Preheat the grill until hot. Grill the bacon rashers until crisp, then drain on kitchen paper. When they are cool enough to handle, break into bite-sized pieces. Break the fish into bite-sized flakes.

Whip the cream until softly stiff, then fold into the horseradish purée.

Place the salad leaves in a large bowl with the parsley, and toss with about half the horseradish dressing and a little seasoning.

Divide the salad mixture between serving plates. Arrange the fish and bacon on top, spoon over the remainder of the dressing, then sprinkle over the chives. Drizzle each serving with a little olive oil and serve immediately.

Serving note This salad is best served with slices of a light rye bread.

Caesar Salad

The basis of a good Caesar salad is the Parmesan. If you can get it, use Parmigiano Reggiano. Its superb flavour comes from the ageing process. While I was working in Italy I cooked with Parmesan that was six years old. Cheaper and younger grana cheeses of Parmesans are good nonetheless. But do not use the powdered stuff they call Parmesan, sold on the same shelf as the real McCoy. This is a foul travesty and should be banned. The dressing for this salad is very special because the garlic is cooked in wine first; this gives it a subtle flavour. And please, when making this salad, don't subject it to the common treatment of cutting everything into incredibly small pieces. Salad ingredients should be seen and not blended into obscurity.

SERVES 4

4 garlic cloves, peeled

150ml (¼ pint) white wine

4 rashers streaky bacon, cut into lardons

2 slices white bread, cut into chunky dice

25g (1oz) butter

2 lettuces, preferably cos

4 egg yolks

2 canned anchovy fillets

55g (2oz) Parmesan, freshly grated

300ml (½ pint) vegetable oil

1 tbsp Dijon mustard

sea salt and freshly ground black pepper

Place the garlic in a pan with the wine, bring to the boil and gently simmer for about 5 minutes until the cloves are soft.

Using two pans, crisp the bacon in one, without fat, and cook the bread in the butter in the other, until golden brown. Drain both on kitchen paper.

Remove the leaves from the lettuces, wash and dry well, then cut into chunky pieces.

Using a blender, mix the wine and garlic with the egg yolks, anchovy fillets and cheese. Keep blending, adding the oil slowly to stop the mix from splitting. (This shouldn't happen as the cheese will make everything blend together more easily.) Then add the mustard, and season with salt and pepper to taste.

Throw all the ingredients into a bowl, mix together and munch away.

A great speedy topping for toast that can double up as a starter or as a garnish for a simple piece of roast cod. Puréed, it's also good as a dip, or stirred into some hot cooked pasta. With so many varieties of tomato around these days, it's difficult to know what to choose. A real tomato rule of thumb is that fruit grown in hot countries, particularly those grown outside, will have much more flavour. Tomatoes sold or ripened on the vine may be more expensive, but they too will taste better because they have not been artificially ripened after picking.

Antipasto of Plum and Sun-dried Tomatoes

SERVES 4

1 x 200g jar sun-dried tomatoes in oil

4 fresh plum tomatoes, quartered

½ red onion, peeled and thinly sliced

2 garlic cloves, peeled and thinly sliced

1 tbsp pesto

15g (½oz) fresh basil

sea salt and freshly ground black pepper

Tip the sun-dried tomatoes into a pan. Add the fresh tomato quarters, onion, garlic and pesto.

Place on the heat to warm gently for 1 minute only. If you cook it for too long it will turn into a mush.

Remove from the heat. Tear the basil into pieces and add to the tomatoes. Season and serve. What could possibly be quicker?

This is very easy to make and is a good dip for a drinks party. It uses sun-dried tomatoes instead of olives, which is ideal for those who, like me, don't like olives. But it can be used in the same way as a traditional tapenade: as a spread, a stuffing, or an addition to sauces. It's good with lamb, chicken and fish.

Sun-dried Tomato Tapenade with Breadsticks

SERVES 4

1 x 400g jar sun-dried tomatoes in oil

1 tbsp capers

2 canned anchovy fillets

1 tbsp pesto

1 tbsp pine kernels

olive oil (if necessary)

sea salt and freshly ground black pepper

TO SERVE
1 packet thin breadsticks

Place all the ingredients into a food processor, except for the olive oil (but including the oil from the tomatoes). Blend until smooth. If there is enough oil from the tomatoes you shouldn't need any extra, but add a little more olive oil if the mixture seems too dry.

Turn into a bowl and serve on a dish surrounded by breadsticks.

Fishmongers often sell lovely plump king scallops ready cleaned. They are rather pricey, but worth it for every deliciously sweet mouthful, and you need only about three per head for this salad. Salted capers, which are available in jars, add a feisty dimension to the green salad, and deep-fried sage leaves provide the final flourish.

Scallop Salad with Salted Capers and Crispy Sage

SERVES 4

12 fresh king scallops, prepared, with corals left on

200g (7oz) rocket leaves

100g (3½oz) watercress

a large handful of fresh flat-leaf parsley

sunflower oil, for deep-frying

8 large fresh sage leaves

1 tbsp olive oil

15g (½oz) butter

2–3 tbsp salted capers

sea salt and freshly ground black pepper

DRESSING

3 tbsp olive oil

juice of 1 large lemon

½ large red chilli, deseeded and chopped

2 garlic cloves, peeled and chopped

Check that the scallops have been thoroughly cleaned and remove any thin black threads. Pat dry with kitchen paper and set aside.

Toss the rocket and watercress together in a large bowl. Remove the leaves from the parsley sprigs and add to the bowl.

Heat the sunflower oil to a depth of about 1cm (½in) in a shallow pan. When the oil is hot enough for a haze to be detected rising from it, add the sage leaves one at a time and deep-fry for 1 minute until just translucent. Drain on kitchen paper. Remember to turn off the heat under the oil pan as soon as you have finished, for safety's sake.

For the dressing, whisk the oil with the lemon juice, chilli, garlic and seasoning. Toss the salad leaves with the dressing, season and divide between four serving plates.

Heat a large non-stick frying pan until you feel a good heat rising. Add the olive oil, then the scallops and fry for about 2 minutes on each side, seasoning well. Do not overcook, or they will become tough. Add the butter and allow the scallops to soak up the buttery pan juices. Arrange on the salad and scatter over the capers. Grind over more pepper, top with the crispy sage leaves and serve immediately.

Pan-fried Mozzarella Wrapped in Bacon with Chutney and Sesame Seeds

This has always been very popular in my restaurants. My friends are keen on it too. One particular friend is always asking me to make it at his house, normally between three and four in the morning. As I'm never quite sober at that time, the fact that this recipe is easy is a point considerably in its favour. Buy speck bacon, or Serrano ham instead, from delicatessens. Whichever you use, make sure it is cooked until crispy. And be sure to use buffalo mozzarella, not one made from cows' milk, for maximum flavour.

SERVES 2

1 x 150g (5½oz) ball of buffalo mozzarella cheese

4 slices speck bacon

4 tbsp olive oil

100g (3½oz) mixed salad leaves

1 tbsp balsamic vinegar

2 tsp sesame seeds, toasted

sea salt and freshly ground black pepper

PLUM CHUTNEY

25g (1oz) butter

8 plums, stoned and chopped

2 tbsp caster sugar

3 tbsp balsamic vinegar

Make the chutney in the morning. Melt the butter and sauté the plums for 2–3 minutes. Add the sugar and vinegar and simmer for 15–20 minutes until the plums are soft and the sauce is rich and sticky.

Open the packet of cheese, drain, and cut the cheese into 4 pieces. Wrap each piece in a slice of speck and secure with wooden cocktail sticks.

Heat half the olive oil in a non-stick pan until very hot. Season the wrapped mozzarella and fry for a few minutes on each side to brown and crisp the bacon.

Place the salad leaves in a bowl with the remaining olive oil, the vinegar and some seasoning and mix. Divide between two plates in a high pile.

Remove the mozzarella from the pan once the speck is nice and crisp and place on top of the salad. Sprinkle with the toasted sesame seeds and pour over the juices remaining in the pan. Add the chutney to the side of each salad and serve.

Tip To toast sesame seeds, put them in a dry pan with no oil and place on a moderate heat. Keep them moving in the pan to avoid burning. Toasting the seeds under a grill is not a good idea as they tend to burst open and pop all over the place.

Salade Niçoise

I worked, sweated and suffered in the worst kitchen in the world to get this and about another ten recipes. The head chef of this particular French restaurant was an honorary member of the Raving Nutcase Society. His kitchen was the type of place the SAS go to train in the art of 'if you can't teach them in a day, beat it into them'. However, credit where credit's due: he did create some decent dishes.

SERVES 2

60g (2¼oz) baby spinach leaves

10 black olives

3 hard-boiled eggs, shelled and quartered

1 x 150g can tuna in oil, drained

8 cooked new potatoes

85g (3oz) cooked French beans

3 tomatoes

2 sprigs fresh basil

olive oil, for drizzling

sea salt and freshly ground black pepper

DRESSING

40g (1½oz) Parmesan

2 egg yolks

1 tbsp white wine vinegar

1 tsp Dijon mustard

2 canned anchovy fillets

1 garlic clove, peeled and chopped

100ml (3½fl oz) olive oil

To make the dressing, take the cheese and, using a peeler, peel about 6 shavings off. Then grate the rest. Place the grated cheese in a small blender with the egg yolks, vinegar, mustard, anchovy fillets and garlic and blend to a paste. While mixing, pour the olive oil slowly into the blender until the dressing is thick. Season and leave to one side.

Rip the spinach leaves roughly into a large bowl and add the olives, eggs and drained tuna. Cut the potatoes into wedges and place in the bowl with the beans. Cut the tomatoes into 6 pieces each, and add, along with some salt and pepper.

Mix the dressing into the salad and season well. Divide between two plates and garnish with the cheese shavings, sprigs of fresh basil and a drizzle of olive oil before serving.

Roasted Red Pepper Hummus

Hummus is a traditional Middle Eastern dip made from chickpeas and sesame tahina, but my variation contains roasted red peppers to give it a different and more interesting flavour. I love red peppers, and don't really use any of the other colours for this recipe as they never seem to taste of anything when puréed. This hummus is very simple to make, and is best served with hot miniature pitta breads, breadsticks or crudités of carrot, celery and red pepper.

SERVES 6

2 x 400g cans chickpeas, drained and rinsed

1 x 400g can or jar roasted red peppers, drained

3 garlic cloves, peeled and chopped

15g (½oz) fresh mint

4–5 tbsp sesame oil

sea salt and freshly ground black pepper

Drain the chickpeas and peppers in a sieve.

Put the chickpeas, peppers, garlic and mint into a food processor and blend until smooth.

Stir in the sesame oil and season to taste with salt and pepper. Spoon into a bowl and serve.

Tip Using canned chickpeas saves time, and once they're puréed they taste no different from cooked dried ones. Canned roasted peppers are available in some supermarkets and good delicatessens.

Charentais Melon, Prosciutto, Wild Rocket and Pecorino Salad

This combination of fruit, meat, salad and cheese highlights the unique partnership of deli ingredients that display pure and different flavours. Simple and quick, this dish will easily satisfy any sweet, salty and tangy cravings.

SERVES 4

2 Charentais melons

24 slices prosciutto

100g (3½oz) wild rocket leaves

200g (7oz) pecorino cheese

3 tbsp extra virgin olive oil

sea salt

Remove the outer skin from the melons. Cut both melons in half and remove the seeds. Slice the melons thinly and arrange on serving plates, together with the sliced prosciutto. Wash and drain the wild rocket and sprinkle a few leaves over the top.

Using a swivel vegetable peeler, shave the pecorino cheese over the salad and drizzle with the olive oil and a little sea salt before serving.

Iberico Ham with a Herby Leaf Salad

Dry-cured and smoked, Spanish hams can be served in the same way as Parma ham – thinly sliced as a starter or buffet dish. Iberico pigs are fed on wild acorns and live a heavenly porcine existence. Consequently the flesh tastes divine and the very dark meat is beautifully flavoured and moist.

SERVES 4

250g (9oz) salad leaves, e.g. wild rocket, red chard, baby spinach

1 tbsp sprigs fresh chervil

2 tbsp fresh flat-leaf parsley leaves

1 tbsp chopped fresh chives

3 tbsp extra virgin olive oil (preferably Spanish)

1 tbsp balsamic or sherry wine vinegar

300g (10½oz) thinly sliced Iberico ham

freshly ground black pepper

Pick over the salad leaves and discard any that are damaged or discoloured. Place in a large bowl and toss with the prepared herbs.

Whisk the oil with the vinegar and seasoning. Pour over the salad leaves and herbs and toss well.

Pile the salad into a mound in the centre of a large platter. Arrange the slices of ham around it, scrunching it loosely into rosettes if desired. Grind over pepper to taste before serving.

Serving note This succulent dish is best served with slices of country-style bread.

OK – let's talk about speck, baby. These rashers of pig belly grill to a sweet, fragrant crispness. You will find two types in delis – Italian speck, which is quite fatty but flavoursome, and the leaner, smokier Spanish variety. Here I've teamed it with small cubes of fine British black pudding, which I also adore. Not for me the sticky slabs found on greasy 'caf' plates. I like my black pudding as it should be – a dark, rich burgundy red, with chunky pieces of creamy fat and a full flavour. Chargrilled artichokes in oil – the other star ingredient of this dish – are one of my favourite store-cupboard standbys.

Crispy Speck, Artichoke and Black Pudding Salad

SERVES 4

125g (4½oz) speck, sliced wafer thin

150g (5½oz) rocket leaves

a small handful of fresh flat-leaf parsley leaves

100g (3½oz) jar chargrilled artichokes in oil, drained and sliced

olive oil, for frying

60g (2¼oz) top-quality black pudding, cut into 1cm (½in) cubes

4 garlic cloves, peeled and roughly crushed

½ small red onion, peeled and thinly sliced

8 cherry tomatoes, halved or whole

Parmesan shavings (optional)

DRESSING

4 tbsp balsamic vinegar

6 tbsp olive oil

sea salt and freshly ground black pepper

Preheat the grill until hot. Grill the speck rashers until crispy, then drain on kitchen paper. Snip into small pieces with kitchen scissors. Set aside.

Whisk the ingredients for the dressing together or place in a screw-top jar and shake to mix. Toss the rocket with the parsley leaves, sliced artichokes and dressing in a large bowl and season well.

Heat a frying pan and, when you feel a steady heat rising, add a trickle of oil, then toss in the black pudding cubes and the garlic. Fry for about 3 minutes until the black pudding is crisp on all sides.

Add the onion and fry for 2 minutes. Add the tomatoes and cook for a further 1–2 minutes. Toss the contents of the pan with the salad and the pieces of speck, check the seasoning and serve immediately. Add a few shavings of Parmesan before serving, if desired.

Variation You could use Spanish serrano ham in place of the speck. For an extra twist, bake the serrano ham slices around a wooden rolling pin in a preheated oven at 190°C/375°F/gas mark 5 for about 10 minutes until crisp. Leave to cool on kitchen paper, then arrange on top of the salad. You can use these as a flamboyant garnish for other dishes, too.

breads
& bread
dishes

Olive Focaccia with Rosemary Oil

Bread-making is easy and can be deeply satisfying, so why not try your hand at making focaccia? This recipe makes two loaves, one of which you could freeze for later use.

MAKES 2 LOAVES, ABOUT 20CM (8IN) IN DIAMETER

500g (1lb 2oz) bread flour, ideally Tipo 2 (*see* Ingredients note)

1 sachet easy-blend yeast

½ tsp sea salt

½ tsp caster sugar

300ml (½ pint) olive oil

300ml (½ pint) tepid water

2 large sprigs fresh rosemary

60g (2¼oz) pitted black olives, chopped

sea salt flakes, for sprinkling (*see* Ingredients note)

It is easier to make this bread in an electric mixer with a dough hook, or in a strong food processor, than by hand. Sift the flour, yeast, salt and sugar into the mixer or food processor bowl. Alternatively, sift the flour, yeast, salt and sugar into a large mixing bowl.

Add 2 tbsp of the oil. Gradually mix in the water until a soft but not too sticky dough forms, with the machine running on a slow speed or using your hands. You may not need all the water, or you may need extra, so add with care. Continue to beat for 5–10 minutes until the dough is smooth and elastic or knead the dough on a lightly floured surface for about 10 minutes.

Place the dough in a lightly oiled bowl and cover loosely with clingfilm, allowing room for expansion. Leave to rise (prove) in a warm place (such as an airing cupboard or near a central-heating boiler) until doubled in size. This can take 30 minutes or up to 2 hours, depending on how warm it is.

Meanwhile, heat the remaining oil gently in a small saucepan and add the rosemary. Remove the pan from the heat and leave to allow the flavour to infuse.

Knock back the dough by punching it down with your fist and knead by hand on a lightly floured surface for a few minutes. Divide in half and shape into 2 rounds about 1.5cm (⅝in) thick.

Place each round on a lightly greased baking sheet and cover loosely with clingfilm. Leave to prove for about 20–30 minutes until doubled in size. Meanwhile, preheat the oven to 200°C/400°F/gas mark 6.

Make small indentations with your fingers all over the surface of each loaf. Brush with the rosemary oil, scatter over the olives and sprinkle with sea salt flakes. Bake for 20 minutes until risen and golden brown. Cool on a wire rack.

Ingredients note Track down the special Italian wheat flour known as Tipo 2, a medium-ground, unbleached flour (makes wonderful pizzas, too). Alternatively, use strong bread flour or a mixture of half strong white and brown wheatmeal (not wholemeal) flour to imitate the texture and colour of Tipo 2. Sea salt flakes are a must to create the characteristic crust; I would recommend Maldon as the best brand.

Serving note Either tear the focaccia into pieces or cut into wedges. Serve with any remaining rosemary oil, which you can strain if you like, for dipping. *Bellissimo*!

Smoked Salmon and Basil Bread

This is a great party bread, which you can serve freshly baked and sliced, or spread with a good soft garlic cheese or lashings of fresh unsalted butter. It is especially good with seafood barbecues. When I was a student chef, our college group was sent to work at various restaurants in the Pornic area of the South of France. We knew when we returned to Yorkshire that we would each have to cook a speciality of the region where we had worked, so before we left we all packed whatever special ingredients were needed to take home. Some packed vine twigs, but I took back a sack of T45 flour used by French bakers in the making of their superb bread. What none of us had anticipated was that when our minibus went through customs, the officers viewed a bus-load of scruffy students with great suspicion. We were held while they examined our hash-like vine twigs and stabbed at my sack with its sinister-looking contents of white powder. Eventually, we made it back to our college kitchens and I made a bread very much like this one with that T45 flour. It's a firm favourite now.

MAKES 1 X 1KG (2LB 4OZ) LOAF

250g (9oz) French or Italian bread flour, e.g. T45 or Tipo 2 (see Ingredients note, page 193)

250g (9oz) strong white flour, plus extra for dusting (alternatively, use 500g/1lb 2oz of one of the above flours)

½ tsp sea salt

15g (½oz) fresh yeast or 1 sachet easy-blend yeast

200ml (7fl oz) tepid milk

a good pinch of sugar (if using fresh yeast)

1 tbsp olive oil, plus extra for greasing

5 tbsp tepid water

150g (5½oz) smoked salmon, chopped (you could use trimmings)

4 large leaves fresh basil, chopped

Sift the flours (or flour) and salt together into a large bowl. If using fresh yeast, cream with 2 tbsp of the milk, the sugar and 1 tsp of the flour. Leave until it starts to froth. If using easy-blend yeast, simply stir into the flour.

Blend the oil with the milk and water. Beat the creamed yeast (if using) into the flour, then gradually work in the oil and milk mixture until you have a soft but not too sticky dough. You may not need all the liquid, or you may need to add extra tepid water in cautious dribbles – it depends on the flour.

Work the dough vigorously with your hands until it leaves the side of the bowl, then turn it out on to a lightly floured surface. Knead it back and forth using a scrubbing action, scrunching the dough into a ball and kneading time and time again. It will begin to get smoother and more elastic after 5–10 minutes.

Place the dough in a lightly oiled bowl and cover with loosely with clingfilm, allowing room for expansion. Leave to rise (prove) in a warm place (such as an airing cupboard or near a central-heating boiler) until the dough is doubled in size.

Knock back the dough by punching it with your fist. Knead on a lightly floured surface, gradually working in the smoked salmon and basil with your hands. Shape the dough into a long oval and place it on a lightly oiled non-stick baking sheet. Score 3 slashes in the top and lightly dust with flour. Cover loosely again with clingfilm and leave to prove a second time for about 1 hour until doubled in size.

Preheat the oven to 190°C/375°F/gas mark 5.

Bake the dough for 30–35 minutes until firm on the outside and cooked inside. You can check this by turning the loaf over and knocking the base – it should sound hollow. If it makes a dull thud instead, bake for a further 5 minutes or so.

Cool on a wire rack. When the loaf is cold, slice and enjoy – real, fresh, homemade bread with a wonderful salmon flavour.

Red Onion and Crème Fraîche Pizzas

On occasions, it's well worth making your own pizza base from scratch and keeping the topping simple and delicious. Easy-blend or fast-action yeasts are sold in easy-to-use sachets that you mix straight into flour. This gives you the best of both worlds – a wonderful homemade bread base made in next to no time. Here the base is given a sourdough flavour with the addition of a little rye flour. The pizza is then baked with whole garlic cloves that you can squeeze over the hot and bubbling pizza before you devour it.

SERVES 4

225g (8oz) plain flour

3 tbsp rye flour

a good pinch of sea salt

1 sachet easy-blend yeast

1 tbsp olive oil

about 100ml (3½fl oz) tepid water

TOPPING

25g (1oz) butter

2 tbsp olive oil, plus extra for drizzling

3 large red onions, peeled and thinly sliced

250g (9oz) full-fat crème fraîche (half-fat is too runny)

6 fat garlic cloves, peeled

4 sprigs fresh thyme

sea salt and freshly ground black pepper

Preheat the oven to 200°C/400°F/gas mark 6.

Sift the flours and salt into a large bowl and stir in the yeast. Mix in the oil, then gradually add the water until you have a firm but sticky dough.

Turn the dough out on to a lightly floured surface. Knead well for about 5 minutes until it becomes smooth and elastic. Cover the dough loosely with clingfilm and set aside while you prepare the topping.

Heat the butter with the oil in a frying pan, add the onions and sauté for a good 10 minutes until softened. Leave to cool a little.

Divide the dough into 2 rounds. Roll each round out on a lightly floured surface as thinly as possible – they should be 25–30cm (10–12in) in diameter. Place on lightly greased baking sheets.

Spread the dough tops with the crème fraîche, then cover with the onions and season well. Press 3 whole garlic cloves on top of each pizza and strip the leaves from the thyme sprigs over the top. Drizzle with a little more olive oil.

Bake in the oven for about 15–20 minutes until golden brown. Serve hot and bubbling from the oven, squeezing the soft flesh from the garlic cloves over the top of the pizzas.

Anchovy and Rosemary Pizzas

Packet pizzas often taste rather artificial. However, making your own from scratch can take a lot of time. The compromise is to use ready-made pizza bases. Failing that, use a ciabatta bread which you can split in two. For the topping, choose a homestyle tomato sauce. I like to use one made by the Bay Tree Food Company, but there are some authentic Italian pasta sauces that can double as pizza spreads. Be sure to use buffalo mozzarella for a fine flavour.

SERVES 2

1 ready-made medium-sized pizza base or medium-sized ciabatta

1 x 300g jar tomato pasta sauce (any flavour)

2 x 150g (5½oz) balls of buffalo mozzarella cheese

1 large sprig fresh rosemary

1 x 50g (1¾oz) can salted anchovies, drained if in oil

4 tbsp freshly grated Parmesan

freshly ground black pepper

Preheat the oven to 200°C/400°F/gas mark 6.

Place the pizza base on a large baking sheet. If using ciabatta, split in half widthways with a bread knife and open it up.

Spread the pizza base or ciabatta with the tomato sauce, taking it right up to the edges. Drain the mozzarella, cut into thin slices and arrange over the tomato sauce.

Strip the leaves from the rosemary sprig and snip into small pieces using kitchen scissors. Sprinkle the rosemary over the mozzarella. Layer the anchovy fillets on top, as artistically as you like or simply position them at random, then sprinkle over half the Parmesan.

Grind over some pepper and bake in the oven for 10–15 minutes until the cheese starts to bubble. Serve with the remaining Parmesan sprinkled over. Eat when piping hot and most delicious.

Mozzarella and Parmesan Pizza

This is a very simple pizza, which is good eaten with a tomato and basil salad, or cut into wedges or squares and eaten as as finger food. Perhaps it is a bit of a cheat using a bought base, but the end result tastes just the same. However, it is important to use the mozzarella made from buffalo milk that comes in whey in a plastic bag. It is creamier and richer than the cows' milk versions, which can be a little rubbery and bland, and it has a far superior flavour.

SERVES 2

1 ready-made 35cm (14in) medium-thickness pizza base

100g (3½oz) Parmesan, freshly grated

200g (7oz) buffalo mozzarella cheese

olive oil, for drizzling

rock salt and freshly ground black pepper

Preheat the oven to 220°C/425°F/gas mark 7.

Using a sharp knife, carefully cut the pizza base in half horizontally to make 2 thin, round pizza bases.

Sprinkle the grated Parmesan evenly over the 2 bases. Drain the mozzarella, cut it into thin slices and arrange on the top. Drizzle with olive oil, season well with salt and pepper and place in the oven for about 5–10 minutes until golden brown in colour.

Hot Onion Bread with Garlic and Hand-peeled Tomatoes

Italian tomatoes have the best flavour without doubt, and some are worth paying a few pounds for, even though you may think twice about the cost compared to the canned variety. Pomodoro sammarzano are whole, hand-peeled tomatoes packed in jars with olive oil and fresh basil leaves. These are not tomatoes for cooking. I would advise you to eat them as 'neat' as possible, on wonderful hand-baked bread, such as the onion loaves from the bakers, De Gustibus, in Oxford. Walnut bread would work just as well. This is simple, rustic food that tastes fantastic.

SERVES 4

1 loaf onion bread, thickly sliced

4–5 fat garlic cloves, peeled and chopped

200ml (7fl oz) olive oil

about 8 large fresh basil leaves, roughly chopped or torn

1 x 400g jar pomodoro sammarzano (hand-peeled tomatoes with basil in oil), drained but oil reserved

sea salt flakes (*see* Ingredients note, page 193) and freshly ground black pepper

Preheat the grill until hot. Lay the bread slices on the grill rack. Whisk the garlic and oil together, then spoon over the bread, coating well.

Grill the bread until pale golden on both sides and divide between four serving plates. Scatter over the fresh basil.

Spoon the tomatoes on to each plate and crush sea salt flakes on top, then grind over the pepper. Let each diner squash his or her tomatoes on to the toasted bread.

Roasted Garlic and Olive Oil Bread

I believe in letting guests help themselves when they come to my home. It makes life easier for me and the evening more relaxing for everyone. This is wonderful food for guests (and host) to nibble while waiting for the rest of the meal to appear. You'll need a couple or more deliciously flavoured loaves of crusty bread, such as walnut or sun-dried tomato, cumin seed or onion.

SERVES 6–8

6–8 large whole bulbs of garlic

250ml (9fl oz) olive oil

3–4 sprigs fresh thyme

2–3 loaves assorted flavoured breads

sea salt flakes (*see* Ingredients note, page 193)

Preheat the oven to 190°C/375°F/gas mark 5.

Cut the garlic bulbs in half widthways and lay on a baking sheet. Drizzle over the oil. Strip the leaves from the thyme sprigs and scatter over the garlic with some crushed sea salt flakes.

Roast in the oven for about 15–20 minutes until the garlic flesh feels soft when pierced with the tip of a knife.

Meanwhile, slice the breads of your choice. If you have time and the facilities for grilling, i.e. a large barbecue or grill pan, you can chargrill the slices and serve as toast.

Transfer the garlic to a serving plate and let your guests scoop out the soft sweet flesh to spread on the bread or toast.

Serving note You can also serve bowls of extra virgin olive oil and pots of sea salt to sprinkle over the garlic-spread bread or toast.

Hot Croissants with Sun-dried Tomatoes and Melted Cheese

This is a good cheap dish, especially when made with slightly stale croissants, sometimes available on the discount shelves of supermarkets. For finger food for a party, cut the filled croissants carefully in half or into chunks or wedges. You can use any cheese that goes runny when cooked. Camembert or Taleggio would be suitable. Camembert is widely available, but you might have to look a little harder for the Italian soft cows' milk cheese, Taleggio. It has a pinky-orange rind, is a little like brie in texture and is well worth searching for. Serve the croissants on their own or, if you're feeling hungry, with some grilled streaky bacon. Then lock the door and eat all four croissants yourself. I do!

SERVES 4

4 croissants

¼ red onion, peeled and chopped

1 garlic clove, peeled and chopped

2 field mushrooms, sliced

25g (1oz) butter

8 sun-dried tomatoes in oil, drained

2 tbsp chopped fresh parsley

25g (8oz) cheese, sliced (*see* recipe introduction)

sea salt and freshly ground black pepper

Preheat the oven to 180°C/350°F/gas mark 4.

Cut the croissants in half horizontally and place the bottoms on an ovenproof tray, leaving the tops to one side.

Sauté the onion, garlic and mushrooms in the butter for about 1 minute, then add the tomatoes and the parsley. Season well.

Spread the onion mix on the 4 croissant bottoms on the tray, top with the cheese and put the 4 croissant lids on top. Place in the oven for 3–4 minutes just to warm through lightly and melt the cheese.

Camembert and Garlic Bread

Some people say garlic is the root of all evil. But, for me, garlic is heaven. This recipe can be made in the 'proper' chef's way using a good-quality bread plus butter and garlic; or the cheat's way with ready-made garlic bread. To be honest, though, there isn't much difference in the time taken: 'cheating' just involves less work. Sourdough is the best bread for this recipe. The bread is raised by a leaven of flour and water that is left to ferment, utilizing natural yeasts in the flour to create gases which raise the dough and give it a unique sour flavour. If you can't find any good sourdough, use pain de campagne, a French-style bread available from most supermarkets.

SERVES 4

1 large oven-ready garlic baguette or 4 thick slices fresh sourdough bread

2 garlic cloves, peeled and finely chopped

115g (4oz) butter, softened (if using sourdough bread)

175g (6oz) Camembert cheese, sliced

Cheat's method Take the oven-ready garlic bread and bake in the oven following the instructions on the packet (normally for about 10 minutes, at about 180°C/350°F/gas mark 4). Remove from the oven, cover with slices of the cheese, and place under a preheated grill until the cheese just melts. Don't worry if the edges burn: they're the best bits.

Sourdough method Mix the garlic with the butter. Toast the sourdough (or French) bread, then spread the garlic butter on it. Cover with cheese as above, and grill until the cheese has just melted.

Gedi Goats' Cheese Bruschetta with Quince and Parma Ham

This may sound like a dish from a *Star Wars* bistro, but in fact gedi goats' cheese is a fine example of one of the many exciting new English cheeses being made today. I've give it a fusion-food twist and served it Mediterranean style with Spanish membrillo quince paste wrapped in Parma ham, which has been quickly pan-fried and caramelized. May the force of flavour be with you!

SERVES 4

150g (5½oz) Spanish membrillo or Portuguese marmelo quince paste

4 slices Parma ham

4 slices ciabatta bread

olive oil, for brushing and frying

2 good pinches of dried thyme or leaves stripped from 2 fresh sprigs

1 fat garlic clove, peeled and halved

300g (10½oz) gedi goats' cheese log or another semi-soft chèvre, rinded and sliced

freshly ground black pepper

Preheat the oven to 200°C/400°F/gas mark 6.

Meanwhile, cut the quince paste into 4 equal-sized slices, then wrap each quince slice in a slice of parma ham. Set aside.

Brush the bread with oil and bake in the oven for 10 minutes until lightly crisp and golden brown.

Meanwhile, heat a trickle of oil in a frying pan and swirl to coat the surface. Add the ham-wrapped quince paste and pan-fry for about 2 minutes on each side until just browned, scattering lightly with the thyme.

Remove the bread from the oven and quickly rub the surface with the garlic, then top with the cheese. Place a ham and quince slice on top of each bread slice and drizzle over any pan juices. Season with pepper and serve immediately.

Serving note This dish is best served with a mixed leaf salad lightly dressed with olive oil and balsamic vinegar.

As my mother would say, this is just poncey cheese on toast. However, to make a more sophisticated snack you could cut the mushrooms into smaller pieces, cook them as below, spoon into bought savoury tartlet cases, top with the cheese and warm through in the oven.

Garlic Mushrooms and Taleggio Cheese on Toast

SERVES 2

2 garlic cloves, peeled and crushed

55g (2oz) butter

15g (½oz) Italian herbs, chopped

4 large field mushrooms, sliced

grated zest and juice of 1 lemon

2 slices white bloomer bread, toasted

55g (2oz) Taleggio cheese

chopped fresh thyme (optional)

sea salt and freshly ground black pepper

Mix the garlic, butter and Italian herbs together, and place in a hot pan with the sliced mushrooms. Season well. Cook quickly as the mushrooms tend to leak a lot of water otherwise. Add the lemon zest and juice.

Spread on the toasted bread. Top with the cheese and grill until the cheese is just melted. Serve hot with some chopped fresh thyme if you have any. Cut into quarters to serve as chunky canapés.

Tip The pan must be really hot when cooking the mushrooms, otherwise the water in the mushrooms leaks out, diluting the flavours and making the bread soggy. If the pan does get a bit wet, 2 tbsp fresh breadcrumbs will soak all the liquid up.

Confit of Tomatoes on Toast

I discovered this while working in a palazzo in northern Italy. It's one of the simplest dishes, yet tastes like one of the best, and I lived on it at breakfast time. The mother of the household would cook a half crate of tomatoes at a time in a lovely old tray that had been blackened with many years of use. She used about 2 litres of local olive oil at a time and saved any left-over oil for the following day.

SERVES 2

6 plum tomatoes

1 tbsp fresh thyme leaves

4 garlic cloves, peeled and chopped

extra virgin olive oil

2 slices good Italian bread

rock salt and freshly ground black pepper

Preheat the oven to 220°C/425°F/gas mark 7.

Place the tomatoes in a small ovenproof dish and sprinkle with the thyme and rock salt. Add the garlic, season with pepper and fill the dish with olive oil, a quarter way up the tomatoes. Bake in the oven for 8–10 minutes.

Drizzle the bread with olive oil and rock salt, and toast it under the grill or in a griddle pan. Spoon the tomatoes from the dish on to the bread, with plenty of olive oil.

Poppy Seed Snaps

This recipe bakes to a thin unleavened bread, which you can break into jagged wafers for serving with pâtés, such as Brandade of Salt Cod (see page 60), or simply with a creamy cheese.

MAKES ABOUT 250G (9OZ)

200g (7oz) bread flour, ideally Tipo 2 (*see* Ingredients note, page 193)

a good pinch of salt

100–150ml (3½–5fl oz) water

3 tbsp olive oil

50g (1¾oz) poppy seeds

Mix the flour and salt with enough cold water to form a thick dough. You can do this in a food processor.

Pull off a lump of dough the size of a large walnut and feed it through the widest setting of a pasta-rolling machine three or four times. Turn the machine to a thinner setting and feed the dough through again. Do this several times, turning the setting down two more stages as the dough gets smoother and more elastic, as if you were making pasta. Don't crank the machine too enthusiastically, or the dough might break.

Place the dough on a flat baking sheet, brush with oil and sprinkle generously with poppy seeds.

Repeat the process with the remaining dough, a lump at a time, until it is all used up.

Meanwhile, preheat the oven to 190°C/375°F/gas mark 5. Bake the poppy seed-covered dough sheets in batches for about 10 minutes until golden brown. Slide on to a wire rack to cool. When completely cold and brittle, snap into biscuit-sized pieces. Store in airtight containers.

pies,
tarts &
batters

Wafer-thin Tomato, Emmenthal and Grain Mustard Tart

This tart is superb served hot with a dressed salad of spinach or rocket. You can also use other toppings that are suggested below. I'm a great believer in saving time in cooking, and ready-prepared filo and puff pastries are great products for quick and tasty dishes. Both are actually better bought fresh (in delicatessens, ethnic shops and some supermarkets). Frozen filo tends to flake a bit in preparation, unless you cover it with a damp tea-towel, and use melted butter.

SERVES 2

150g (5½oz) filo pastry, thawed if frozen

olive oil, for brushing and drizzling

3 tbsp grain mustard

55g (2oz) Emmenthal cheese, sliced

6 tomatoes, sliced

sea salt and freshly ground black pepper

TO SERVE

2 tbsp balsamic vinegar

5 tbsp olive oil

100g (3½oz) rocket or baby spinach leaves

a little basil pesto sauce

Preheat the oven to 230°C/450°F/gas mark 8.

Lay a sheet of pastry on a baking sheet, brush it with a little olive oil, then put another sheet on top. Keep adding sheets in this way.

When you have built up about 12–15 layers of pastry, spread the top with the mustard and lay the cheese over it. Place the tomato slices all over the top of the tart, overlapping them as you go.

Season well, drizzle with olive oil and bake in the oven for 15 minutes until the pastry base is cooked. Remove from the oven.

In a bowl, mix the balsamic vinegar with the olive oil and some salt and pepper. Combine the salad leaves with the dressing.

Remove the tart from the tray and drizzle with the pesto. Serve with the dressed salad.

Tip There is a number of alternative toppings. Why not try smoked salmon, red onion and crème fraîche; wild mushrooms, thyme and mozzarella cheese; figs and Gorgonzola cheese; or spinach, crème fraîche and shelled mussels?

Lobster, Mango and Rocket Tarts

This is a really glamorous starter yet deceptively easy to make; the pastry cases are quickly made from ready-to-use filo pastry (you will find a 4-hole Yorkshire pudding tin useful here). Make sure that everything is prepared and waiting to be assembled just before serving.

SERVES 4

4–6 large sheets filo pastry, thawed if frozen (*see* Ingredients note)

about 50g (1¾oz) butter, melted

1 whole cooked lobster, about 500g (1lb 2oz)

1 large mango, ripe but not soft

4 tbsp Citrus and Vanilla Dressing (*see* page 286)

1 tbsp olive oil

2 tsp balsamic vinegar

about 100g (3½oz) rocket leaves

4 large fresh basil leaves, finely chopped

sea salt and freshly ground black pepper

Cut the filo pastry into 20 x 15cm (6in) squares. Keep the cut squares under a clean damp tea towel to prevent them drying out too quickly.

Brush each square quickly and lightly with the melted butter and place one in each hole of a 4-hole Yorkshire pudding tin or 4 individual tartlet tins about 10cm (4in) in diameter. Add 4 more squares, one at a time, to each hole or tin, placing each square at a slightly different angle from the one before, to form a crown shape. Make sure that the pastry is well pressed into the sides of the holes or tins. Chill in the refrigerator until ready to bake.

Preheat the oven to 180°C/350°F/gas mark 4. Crack the shell of the lobster and extract the cooked flesh from the tail and claws. Cut into neat pieces.

Place the lobster meat on a non-stick baking sheet. Peel the mango thinly and cut the flesh into long neat slices. Place on the baking sheet with the lobster and brush with half the Citrus and Vanilla Dressing. Set aside.

Bake the filo pastry cases in the oven for about 10–12 minutes until crisp and lightly golden. Allow to cool before carefully lifting from the tins and transferring to a wire rack to cool completely.

Meanwhile, whisk the oil with the vinegar. Add to the rocket leaves with some seasoning and toss well. Place the mango and lobster in the oven to heat through for about 5 minutes.

Fill the tarts with the mango, lobster, rocket and basil. Drizzle over the remainder of the Citrus and Vanilla Dressing, season and serve immediately.

No one likes waste, and I love inventing recipes at home which use up left-over pieces of meat or fish. This is an ideal way of using up salmon (or you can buy cooked salmon fillets in most supermarkets). Tartlet cases are not essential; you could just spread the rillettes on some hot toast for a great finger-food snack.

Tartlets of Salmon Rillettes with Coriander

MAKES 24 TARTLETS

140g (5oz) cooked salmon, without skin and bone

55g (2oz) butter, softened

¼ red onion, peeled and finely diced

½ red pepper, deseeded and finely diced

1 garlic clove, peeled and finely diced

15g (½oz) fresh coriander, chopped

1 packet (usually containing 24) small savoury tartlet cases

sea salt and freshly ground black pepper

Flake the salmon flesh in a bowl. Mix it with the softened butter, onion, red pepper and garlic. Season well with salt and black pepper. Add the chopped coriander.

Mix well and spoon into the tartlets. Serve fairly quickly as the tartlet cases will soften.

Tip The salmon mixture can be made the day before and stored in the fridge, but remove well before serving to allow it to soften slightly before spooning into the tartlet cases.

Picos blue is a creamy Spanish blue cheese that bakes beautifully as a tart filling. I like to team it with caramelized onions, which you can buy ready-made in the form of a relish or chutney. The best is produced by the Bay Tree Food Company. If you can, use a balsamic vinegar that is at least eight years old for the dressing. It will reward you with a more mellow flavour.

Picos Blue and Caramelized Onion Tarts

MAKES 4 INDIVIDUAL TARTS

500g (1lb 2oz) frozen puff or shortcrust pastry, thawed

250g (9oz) Picos blue cheese, rind removed

90g (3¼oz) mascarpone cheese

2 large egg yolks

leaves stripped from 1 sprig fresh thyme

175g (6oz) caramelized onion relish or chutney

frilly salad leaves, to serve

sea salt and freshly ground black pepper

DRESSING

90g (3¼oz) sun-dried tomatoes in oil, drained and finely chopped, plus 1 tbsp oil from the jar

1 tbsp chopped fresh dill

2 tbsp good-quality, aged balsamic vinegar

2 tbsp extra virgin olive oil

1 small garlic clove, peeled and crushed

1 small shallot, peeled and finely chopped

Roll out the pastry on a lightly floured surface to the thickness of a £1 coin and cut out 4 rounds 13cm (5in) in diameter. Use to line a 4-hole Yorkshire pudding tin or 4 individual tartlet tins about 10cm (4in) in diameter. Prick the bases all over with a fork and place in the refrigerator for about 20 minutes to rest.

Preheat the oven to 200°C/400°F/gas mark 6.

The tarts are best baked 'blind' first. Line each pastry case with foil, add baking beans and set the tins on a metal baking sheet. Bake for 12–15 minutes, remove the foil and beans and return to the oven for a further 5 minutes if the pastry still looks a little raw.

Meanwhile, beat the blue cheese and mascarpone thoroughly until creamy, then mix in the egg yolks, thyme leaves, freshly ground pepper and a little salt.

Remove the tarts from the oven and reduce the heat to 180°C/350°F/gas mark 4. Spoon 1 scant tbsp relish or chutney into each tart base, then top with the cheese mixture. Return to the oven and bake for about 15 minutes until the filling is just set.

Meanwhile, to make the dressing, whisk the chopped tomatoes with the reserved oil, add the remaining ingredients and season to taste.

Place the tarts on small serving plates with an extra dollop of caramelized onion relish or chutney on the side. Drizzle the dressing around each tart, grind over some black pepper and add a leaf or two of frilly lettuce to serve.

Granny knows best, especially when making Yorkshire puddings. However, there are some golden rules to follow: you must cook on a high heat first, then turn the oven down; and you mustn't open the oven door at all for the first 20–25 minutes. And for the best ones, make your mixture a day in advance and leave it to rest in the fridge.

Granny's Yorkshire Pudding with Onions

SERVES 4

225g (8oz) plain flour

8 eggs

600ml (1 pint) milk

55g (2oz) good dripping

sea salt and freshly ground
black pepper

ONIONS

2 white onions, peeled and sliced

250ml (9fl oz) red wine

400ml (14fl oz) fresh beef stock

Place the flour and some seasoning into a bowl. Add the eggs, mixing in with a whisk, and then the milk, mixing slowly to prevent lumps forming. At this point, put the bowl in the fridge overnight covered with some clingfilm.

Preheat the oven to 220°C/425°F/gas mark 7.

Take 4 non-stick Yorkshire pudding tins about 13cm (5in) in diameter. Put a little of the dripping in each of the tins, but don't use it all. Put the tins into the hot oven. Before you add the mix to the tins, the fat in the tins should be smoking hot.

As you pour the mix so that it fills the tins to the top, the mix should seal on the edges. Working fast, place them back in the oven, close the door and leave it closed for about 20–25 minutes.

Meanwhile, cook the onions in a pan in the remaining dripping, for about 10 minutes, then add the wine and stock. Reduce until you have a nice thickened mixture: about another 10 minutes or so. Season well.

Turn the oven down to 190°C/375°F/gas mark 5 and cook the Yorkshires for a further 10 minutes to set the bottom of the puds thoroughly. Remove from the oven, place on plates and serve the thick onion gravy in the middle.

This is a variation on the traditional apple tarte tatin, which is cooked with pastry on top of the fruit, but served upside-down with the fruit – and a delicious caramel – over the pastry. Here I have suggested using six individual 7.5cm (3in) non-stick flan tins, but you could make it in a 20cm (8in) sponge tin, when it would serve four people. You could also use canned pineapple instead of fresh, but see the Tip below.

Pineapple and Black Pepper Tarte Tatin

SERVES 6

200g (7oz) caster sugar

25g (1oz) butter

12 black peppercorns, crushed

6 slices fresh pineapple, peeled and cored

1 x 375g packet pre-rolled puff pastry, thawed if frozen

TO SERVE

500ml (18fl oz) vanilla ice-cream

To make the caramel, put the sugar into a pan and heat gently without stirring until it turns golden brown (*see* page 223 for more information about this process). Remove from the heat, add the butter and stir in gently. Pour this into 6 non-stick flan tins, 7.5cm (3in) in diameter.

Sprinkle the crushed pepper over the caramel and cover with the slices of pineapple (you may need to cut them to fit).

Preheat the oven to to 200°C/400°F/gas mark 6.

Take the puff pastry out of the packet and place on a lightly floured surface. Cut out 6 circles slightly larger than the flan tins. Cover each of the tins with a pastry circle and press the edges down the side of the tins around the edges of the pineapple. Bake in the oven for 15–20 minutes until the pastry is brown.

Remove the tarts from the oven and leave to rest for 2 minutes before turning them out. Place a plate on top of each one and invert so that the tart slips out, pastry to the base, pineapple on the top. Serve hot with the vanilla ice-cream.

Tip If you use canned pineapple instead of fresh, it needs to be drained very thoroughly and dried on kitchen paper before adding to the caramel in the tins. And when removing from the tins, be careful as a lot more juice will have been generated. If there is too much there, before turning out, place the dish back on the heat and cook until the liquid evaporates and the caramel caramelizes again.

Warm Banana Tarte Tartin

This is a very quick and equally delicious tart. Use bananas that have spotty skins for the best flavour and serve with scoops of a good-quality ice-cream (*see* Ingredients note).

SERVES 6–8

500g (1lb 2oz) bought puff pastry, thawed if frozen

250g (9oz) caster sugar

25g (1oz) butter, softened

leaves stripped from 1 sprig fresh rosemary, chopped

6 ripe bananas

Roll out the pastry on a lightly floured surface and cut into a 25cm (10in) round. Prick all over with a fork, then leave to rest in the refrigerator while you make the filling.

Place the sugar in a heavy-based saucepan and melt slowly over a very low heat until it turns a mid-caramel colour. You might like to add 1 tbsp water to help it on its way, but most chefs don't. It is vital not to allow the syrup to bubble even around the edge until all the sugar grains have dissolved, otherwise the mixture will become grainy. It can help to brush the sides of the pan with a pastry brush dipped in cold water, to prevent any stray sugar grains from causing the syrup to crystallize.

As soon as the sugar turns a mid-caramel colour, plunge the pan base into a sink of cold water to halt the browning. It will spit alarmingly, so make sure that your arm is well covered. Beat in the butter until the mixture turns to a buttery caramel. Pour the caramel into an ovenproof frying pan, or 23cm (9in) shallow cake tin, turn and evenly coat the bottom and sides with the caramel.

Preheat the oven to 190°C/375°F/gas mark 5. Sprinkle the chopped rosemary over the surface of the caramel, then slice the bananas on top. Finally, place the pastry round over the sliced bananas, pressing the edge down the sides of the filling all the way round.

Bake in the oven for 20–25 minutes until the pastry is crisp and golden. Remove carefully from the oven to prevent spilling the hot caramel. Allow to stand for a few minutes before carefully inverting on to a serving plate. Cut into wedges to serve.

Ingredients note For a really good bought ice-cream, I would recommend Rocombe Farm.

Serving note If you feel like making some ice-cream to serve with the tart, follow the recipe for Vanilla Ice-cream (*see* page 243), but replace 1 vanilla pod with a 10cm (4in) sprig fresh rosemary.

Lemon tart is highly regarded as a true chef's pudding, but it needs to be good: the pastry should be thin and the filling plentiful, but to do this without it leaking is a bit of a hit-and-miss affair, even for most chefs. While working as a pastry chef at 190 Queens Gate, I probably ruined about ten out of twelve tarts before I found an easy way of making them. My variation uses goats' cheese, which tends to balance some of the sharpness of the lemon juice and, while cooking, melts into the curd mixture.

Lemon and Goats' Cheese Tart with Crème Fraîche

SERVES 4

10 eggs

375g (13oz) caster sugar

500ml (18fl oz) double cream

juice and grated zest of 5 lemons

about 10g (¼oz) butter, softened

225g (8oz) sweet pastry (bought will do)

55g (2oz) Gedi goats' cheese

icing sugar, for dusting

crème fraîche, to serve

To make the filling, crack the eggs into a bowl and whisk gently to break up the yolks. Add the sugar and continue to mix, then add the cream and the juice of the lemons – but not the zest. Pass the mixture through a sieve, then add the zest and leave to one side.

Preheat the oven to 200°C/400°F/gas mark 6.

Grease a 20cm (8in) plain flan ring with the softened butter and place on a baking tray. Roll the pastry out until about 3mm (⅛in) thick. Carefully roll the pastry back on to the rolling pin, place over the ring and unroll very loosely. (If you don't leave plenty of slack, the pastry will rip or shrink too much when cooking.) Carefully tuck the pastry down the sides of the ring, pressing into the bottom edge well, but be careful not to stretch or tear the pastry while doing so. Don't trim the pastry off, but line it with a circle of greaseproof paper that is bigger than the tart. Fill with baking beans, rice or small wooden balls for baking 'blind'.

Place in the oven and bake for about 10 minutes. Remove from the oven, remove the beans and paper, and place the pastry case back in the oven to colour the base. It should only take 3–4 minutes.

Turn the oven down to 140°C/275°F/gas mark 1. Pour the lemon mix into the pastry case, filling it to the top. Crumble the cheese over the tart, put back in the oven and continue to cook for about 1–1½ hours until the filling is only just set.

Remove from the oven, trim off the edges of the pastry and leave the tart to cool for about 2 hours. Dust the tart with plenty of icing sugar and place under a hot grill to caramelize the top. Remove from the grill, cut into wedges and serve with plenty of crème fraîche.

Tip This recipe needs a very mild goats' cheese. I use Gedi, which is English. It should be available from most good delicatessens but, if not, they should be able to order it. It's worth the wait.

Spiced Pear and Apple Danish

Delis are a good source of spices and often stock a better range than the usual limited variety in supermarkets. Allspice, for example, is often not that easy to track down. Also known as Jamaica pepper or pimento, allspice is not another name for mixed spice but a distinct spice in its own right. It's just that our ancestors thought it smelt of all sorts of spices. You can buy the allspice berries whole (great for game stews, pâtés and rich cakes) or in ready-ground form. It is quite pungent, so a pinch is all you need. As with all spices, store in a cool, dark cupboard rather than exposed on a kitchen shelf – spices lose their bouquet and colour in daylight. Remember to check their use-by dates regularly.

MAKES 6

375g (13oz) pack ready-rolled puff pastry, thawed if frozen

25g (1oz) unsalted butter

25g (1oz) caster sugar or unrefined light soft brown sugar

1 large comice pear, peeled, cored and chopped

1 large golden delicious or granny smith apple, peeled, cored and chopped

a good pinch each of ground allspice and cinnamon

1 tsp chopped fresh rosemary leaves

1 egg yolk, beaten with a few drops of water, for glazing

1 tbsp icing sugar

Cut the pastry sheet into 6 squares with sides of 11cm (4¼ in). Make 4 x 4cm (1½in) cuts in each pastry square, 1.5cm (⅝ in) from each outside edge. Prick the inner squares all over with a fork and place on a greased baking sheet. Chill in the refrigerator for 10 minutes.

Meanwhile, to make the filling, melt the butter with the sugar in a saucepan. Stir in the chopped fruit, spices and rosemary. Heat for just 2 minutes or so until the fruit is slightly softened but not cooked. Remove from the heat and leave to cool. Preheat the oven to 190°C/375°F/gas mark 5.

Divide the filling between the pastry squares, spooning it into the centre of each square. Draw the cut borders into the centre of each square and press together with a dab of the egg yolk glaze. Brush all the pastry with the glaze, then bake in the oven for 10 minutes. Remove the pastries from the oven and dust with the icing sugar, shaken from a sieve. Return to the oven to bake for a further 5–10 minutes when the sugar should start to caramelize.

Remove from the oven and, when the pastry is crisp, slide off on to a wire rack to cool.

These must rate as the fastest apple tarts this side of the Wild West, especially now that you can buy ready-rolled puff pastry. Use the Spanish membrillo quince paste or the Portuguese marmelo from a good deli, warming it gently if it is a little too thick to spread. The flavoured whipped cream is a good alternative to nutty ice-cream and melts divinely over the little tarts.

Quince and Apple Tarts with Honey-walnut Cream

MAKES 4

2 x 375g (13oz) packs ready-rolled puff pastry, thawed if frozen

6 golden delicious or granny smith apples, cored

50g (1¾oz) butter, melted

125g (4½oz) membrillo or marmelo quince paste

25g (1oz) caster sugar

HONEY-WALNUT CREAM

150ml (¼ pint) double cream, whipped

2 tbsp clear honey

2 tbsp chopped walnuts

Cut 4 rounds from the 2 sheets of pastry about 15cm (6in) in diameter, using a small side plate or cake tin as a template. Place on 2 baking sheets, prick the bases well with a fork and chill in the refrigerator. Preheat the oven to 200°C/400°F/gas mark 6.

Mix the whipped cream with the honey and nuts and chill in the refrigerator for about 30 minutes until firm.

Meanwhile, cut the apples in half lengthways and slice wafer thin. Brush the edges of the pastry rounds with a little melted butter. Spread the quince paste over the top of the rounds. Arrange the apple slices either in a neat fan shape or in a casual jumble on top. Brush with the remaining melted butter and sprinkle over the sugar.

Bake in the oven for about 15–20 minutes until the pastry edges are crisp and golden brown. Slide the tarts off the baking sheets with a palette knife on to dessert plates. Scoop a smooth oval of honey-walnut cream using a dessert spoon dipped in hot water and place on a tart. Repeat for the other tarts and serve immediately.

Hot Walnut Tart

This easy-to-prepare sweet flan combines bought pastry with a quick-mix filling. Check the use-by date if you are using a pack of shelled walnuts, since they will taste stale if they are ageing – not a problem you will encounter if you buy from a good deli. One little tip: don't overcook the filling. It needs to be served a little gooey, so remove the flan tin from the oven when the mixture is still a little wobbly. Serve with scoops of caramel or toffee ice-cream, or alternatively try it with dollops of rich crème fraîche.

SERVES 6

350g (12oz) pack sweet shortcrust pastry, thawed if frozen

softened butter, for greasing (optional)

FILLING

250g (9oz) light soft brown sugar

225g (8oz) golden syrup

85g (3oz) butter

2 tbsp milk

1 tsp vanilla essence

4 large free-range eggs

300g (10½oz) walnuts, halved or chopped

Roll out the pastry on a lightly floured surface to fit a 23cm (9in) loose-based flan tin. If desired, you can lightly grease the flan tin first, but this is not necessary with most pastries. It does, however, make the pastry bake to a more golden colour.

Lay the pastry over the flan tin and press well into the base of the tin, bringing it up and over the sides. Leave untrimmed. Prick the base a few times with a fork and chill in the refrigerator for 30 minutes. Meanwhile, preheat the oven to 190°C/375°F/gas mark 5.

Line the flan case with a large sheet of foil and baking beans, place on a baking sheet and bake 'blind' in the oven for 15 minutes.

Remove the foil and beans, trim the pastry edges with a sharp knife so that they are neat, then return the flan case to bake for a further 5 minutes. Leave to cool while you make the filling. Reduce the oven temperature to 180°C/350°F/gas mark 4.

Heat the sugar, syrup and butter together in a saucepan until just blended, then remove from the heat and stir in the milk and vanilla. Leave to cool for 5 minutes, then beat the eggs and add to the syrupy liquid.

Scatter the nuts over the flan case and pour over the liquid filling. Return the flan to the oven and bake for 40–45 minutes until set but still a little soft in the centre – make sure that the top doesn't over-brown or burn. Remove from the oven and cool before pushing up the base of the flan tin to unmould the flan.

Variation You could use pecans in place of walnuts for a sweeter flavour.

Banana and Allspice Tart with Honey-walnut Cream

Bring this together at the very last moment, although the pastry circles could have been baked in advance (the day before, for instance). It'll take minutes only, while the tea or coffee is brewing, or your companion is squeezing some fresh orange juice. Allspice is one of the great spices in cooking. It seems to combine the flavours of cinnamon, nutmeg and cloves and is often used in Caribbean food. It goes really well with bananas. The honey-walnut cream is used instead of ice-cream, but when made should be put in the fridge and served with a hot spoon.

SERVES 2

350g (12oz) pack frozen sweet pastry, thawed

5 bananas, peeled

2 tbsp ground allspice

icing sugar

2 sprigs fresh mint

HONEY-WALNUT CREAM

100ml (3½fl oz) double cream, whipped

50ml (2fl oz) clear honey

55g (2oz) shelled walnuts, chopped

Preheat the oven to 180°C/350°F/gas mark 4.

Roll out the pastry to 5mm (¼in) thickness, and cut into 4 circles of 15cm (6in) diameter. Bake in the oven for about 15 minutes, or until just brown on the edges only. Remove from the oven and allow to cool.

Dice 2 of the bananas, mix with the ground allspice and layer half of this mixture between 2 of the pastry circles. Make a second tart in the same way, using the other 2 circles of pastry.

Slice the remaining bananas, place the sliced banana on the top layers of pastry and dust with icing sugar. Caramelize on the top with a blow torch (or under a preheated grill).

Whip the cream to soft peaks, then mix with the honey and nuts. Spoon on top of the caramelized pastry and banana, and garnish with fresh mint before serving.

Super-light Pancakes

We don't make pancakes often enough in this country, which is a great shame when they make such good, quick, hot desserts. I like to serve mine with fresh fruit – especially raspberries – ice-cream and some rich syrup trickled over, such as the Selsey Company's Vanilla Syrup. Alternatively, you could try light maple syrup.

**MAKES ABOUT
8 PANCAKES, TO SERVE 4**

175g (6oz) self-raising flour

2 tsp baking powder

125g (4½oz) caster sugar

2 eggs

½–1 tsp vanilla essence (optional)

250ml (9fl oz) milk

softened butter or sunflower oil, or both, for cooking

Sift the flour and baking powder into a large bowl, stir in the sugar and make a well in the centre.

Break the eggs into a clean bowl and add the vanilla essence (if using) and 2 tbsp of the milk. Make a well in the dry ingredients and pour in the egg mixture. Using a whisk, gradually draw the dry ingredients into the egg mixture, adding the remaining milk gradually as you whisk. Eventually, you should have a slightly lumpy batter. Don't over-mix the batter or it will make the pancakes heavy.

Heat a heavy-based non-stick frying pan until you feel a good heat rising. Add a small knob of butter and/or trickle in a little oil. Spoon 2–3 tbsp of the batter into the pan. (If you want nice neat edges, you could stand an 8cm (3¼in) round metal cutter in the pan to contain the batter. The resulting pancakes will resemble crumpets.)

Cook until bubbles rise to the surface and the batter becomes firm. Loosen from the bottom of the pan and flip over for a few seconds to brown the other side.

Repeat with the remaining batter, stacking the hot pancakes under a clean tea-towel until ready to serve.

Hot Pancakes with Black Cherries, Berries and Vodka

To make pancakes, you need to use a heavy sauté pan, through which the heat will be conducted well. Fussy chefs say you should make the batter and then rest it before cooking, but I think this rule only really applies to Yorkshire pudding batter. Here, as the mix doesn't need to rise, there's no point in resting it. Another piece of advice is to make the pancakes with as little oil as possible.

SERVES 2

115g (4oz) plain flour

1 egg and 1 egg yolk

300ml (½pint) milk

2 tbsp oil

SAUCE

140g (5oz) black cherries

140g (5oz) blackberries
(or raspberries)

2 tbsp caster sugar

juice and grated zest of 1 orange

2 tbsp cassis

4 tbsp vodka

TO SERVE

100g (3½oz) crème fraîche

To start the pancake mix, sift the flour into a bowl and add the egg and egg yolk. Beat to mix before pouring the milk in slowly. This should prevent lumps forming.

Once the mix is smooth, heat a heavy sauté pan, crêpe pan or non-stick frying pan on the stove with a drip of oil in the bottom. Spoon either a small ladleful of the mix into the pan, or just enough to cover the base of the pan. As you put it in, lift the pan and move it in a circular fashion to ensure a thin layer of mix over the entire bottom. Return to the heat and colour on one side: about 2 minutes only. Turn or flip over and colour the other side: another couple of minutes. Remove the pancake from the pan and fold it in half and then in half again. Keep warm under foil on a large plate.

Continue to make more pancakes in the same way until all the mixture is gone. Keep them warm under the foil.

To make the sauce, put the cherries, blackberries, sugar, orange juice and zest into a pan. Place on a moderate heat and warm gently until the blackberries start to break up and so create a sauce in the bottom of the pan.

In a separate small pan quickly warm up the cassis and vodka, then flame them to remove the alcohol. As the flames die down, pour into the fruity sauce.

Uncover the pancakes and pour the hot sauce over them. To finish, spoon the crème fraîche on top and allow it to melt slightly before you serve.

eggs, cream & vanilla

Vanilla Crème Brûlée

This is without question the best recipe I have ever used. I got it when I was working my way around Europe as a teenager, cooking in various restaurants with crazy chefs. This was one of only a small batch of recipes I managed to pick up along the way. A good crème brûlée needs care, fresh vanilla pods, and a long time in the oven.

SERVES 6

8 egg yolks

115g (4oz) caster sugar

2 vanilla pods, split lengthways and seeds removed, seeds and pod reserved

750ml (1 pint 6fl oz) double cream

250ml (9fl oz) milk

55g (2oz) demerara sugar

Preheat the oven to 140°C/275°F/gas mark 1.

Place the egg yolks and caster sugar in a bowl and add the vanilla seeds and pod. Using a whisk, gently combine the mixture, then slowly stir in the cream and milk.

Pass the mix through a sieve and divide between 6 small ovenproof dishes or ramekins about 9cm (3½in) in diameter and 2.5cm (1in) deep. Place in the oven and cook for about 1½–2 hours until set on the top. To check if the mixture is cooked, move the dishes. If it still ripples, it's not ready. (But overcooking will cause the brûlée to crack on the top once cooked, so be careful.)

Remove from the oven, and place in the fridge until set, normally about an hour.

Dust the surface with the demerara sugar and either blow-torch or grill until golden brown. Serve.

Panna Cotta

The Italians certainly do have some lovely desserts, and this is one of them. It is a rich, creamy, orange and vanilla jelly that you can make earlier in the day and serve chilled with Spiced Oranges (see the recipe on page 272).

SERVES 8

2 oranges

1.2 litres (2 pints) double cream

2 vanilla pods, split lengthways and seeds removed, seeds and pods reserved

150g (5½oz) caster sugar

4 leaves gelatine or 1 sachet gelatine crystals

125ml (4fl oz) milk

5 tbsp vodka

Grate the zest of the oranges. Place in a deep non-stick saucepan with 800ml (1 pint 7fl oz) of the cream, the vanilla seeds and pods and the sugar. Bring to the boil, stirring once or twice, then reduce the heat and simmer until reduced by half. Stir frequently to prevent the bottom of the pan from burning. Remove from the heat.

If using gelatine leaves, place them in a bowl of cold water to soften. When they have softened, remove and set aside on a plate. Heat the milk until almost boiling, remove from the heat and add the soaked gelatine leaves. Stir until dissolved. If using gelatine crystals, sprinkle the crystals over the cold milk and allow to soak. Heat over a very low heat until dissolved, stirring once or twice.

Strain the milk through a sieve into the reduced cream mixture, stir and leave to cool. Discard the vanilla pods.

When the cream and gelatine mixture is cold but not quite set, whip the remaining cream and fold into the setting cream together with the vodka. Pour this mixture into a large wet mould of about 1 litre (1¾ pints) capacity or 8 moulds or ramekins of 150ml (¼ pint) capacity. Place in the refrigerator until firmly set.

To serve, turn the panna cotta on to wet serving plates by running a knife around the edge.

Serving note Serve with Spiced Oranges (page 272) and spun sugar. To prepare spun sugar: it is best to use a sugar thermometer. Place 250g (9oz) granulated sugar into a deep saucepan and heat gently until completely dissolved, stirring occasionally. When the mixture reaches 152°C (306°F), immediately remove from the heat and cool for 2 minutes. Rub a wooden rolling pin or steel rod lightly with sunflower oil. Dip a spoon into the syrup and quickly whirl it around the rolling pin. The syrup will form thin strands and will remain pliable for a few seconds so that you can slip it off and lightly shape it as desired.

Lemon, Pine Nut and Brown Breadcrumb Cheesecake

The days of rock-hard cheesecakes topped with soggy canned strawberries are dead and buried, I wish. This recipe is a combination of three different flavours that people wouldn't normally put together in desserts. I love this pudding – which I made up when appearing on *Ready Steady Cook* – as it's so simple and quick. The flavours of the pine kernels and lemon combine so well with the cheese and breadcrumbs, but use only freshly toasted brown breadcrumbs.

SERVES 4

2 egg yolks

4 tbsp caster sugar

6 digestive biscuits

8 tbsp fresh brown breadcrumbs, toasted

25g (1oz) butter, softened

1 tbsp clear honey

juice and grated zest of 2 lemons

1 tbsp pine nuts, toasted

250g (9oz) mascarpone cheese

250ml (9fl oz) double cream, whipped to soft peaks

1 x 250g (9oz) strawberries

Place the egg yolks and sugar into a bowl and whisk very well until light and thick (known as the light ribbon stage).

In another bowl, crush the biscuits finely. Add half the breadcrumbs, and combine with the softened butter and the honey. Place this mixture into 4 metal rings of 7.5cm (3in) diameter on a baking tray, or into a 20cm (8in) spring-form tin, and press evenly over the base.

Add the lemon juice and zest, remaining breadcrumbs and the pine nuts to the egg mixture and mix together with a wooden spoon. Then fold in the cheese carefully followed by the whipped cream, being careful not to mix it too much as this will cause it to split and not set.

Spoon the mix into the rings or tin(s) and, using a palette knife, press it down well to prevent air bubbles. Place in the fridge for about 1 hour to set.

Remove the flan(s) from the rings or tin by wrapping around with a hot cloth to loosen the sides. Place the cheesecake(s) on a plate and decorate with the strawberries before serving.

Make a quick and easy cake mix using almonds and polenta for a nice crunchy texture, then bake on top of a rich butterscotch sauce in which you have sat pineapple rings. Serve with some delicious bought fruit sauces – apricot and raspberry coulis are two of my favourites.

Pineapple and Polenta Cakes with Two Coulis

SERVES 6

150g (5½oz) unsalted butter, softened

1–2 tbsp flour

175g (6oz) caster sugar

425g can pineapple rings in natural juice, drained

100g (3½oz) ground almonds

75g (2½oz) fine polenta

½ tsp baking powder

a good pinch of salt

2 free-range eggs, beaten

juice and grated zest of 1 lemon, to serve

100ml (3½fl oz) ready-made raspberry coulis

100ml (3½fl oz) ready-made apricot coulis

Lightly grease 6 ramekins of 150ml (¼ pint) capacity with a little of the softened butter. Dust the sides with the flour and shake out the excess. Place the ramekins on a baking sheet.

Place 50g (1¾oz) of the sugar in a medium-sized heavy-based saucepan and add 1 tbsp water. Over a very low heat, melt the sugar to a caramel, shaking the pan occasionally. Do not allow it to bubble, even around the edge, until all the grains have dissolved. You may find it helpful to brush the sides of the pan with a pastry brush dipped in cold water, to prevent any stray sugar crystals from causing the syrup to crystallize.

When the sugar has dissolved, raise the heat and allow it to turn a light caramel colour. Using a long-handled wooden spoon, beat in a small knob of the remaining butter, taking care not to burn yourself. Immediately divide the caramel between the 6 prepared ramekins and set a pineapple slice on top.

Preheat the oven to 180°C/350°F/gas mark 4.

Mix together the almonds, polenta, baking powder and salt.

Beat the remaining butter and sugar together until light and creamy. Gradually beat in the eggs, followed by the dry almond and polenta mixture. Finally, beat in the lemon juice and zest.

Spoon the mixture into the ramekins over the top of the pineapple. Level the tops with the back of a teaspoon and bake in the oven for 15–20 minutes until risen and firm to the touch.

Run a table knife around each ramekin and demould carefully on to serving plates. Take care that the hot caramel does not run out on to your hands. Trickle the raspberry and apricot coulis around each pudding.

Serving note Serve with cream or mascarpone on the side. Alternatively, thin the mascarpone with a little pouring cream, sweeten with a little sugar and add 1–2 drops vanilla essence.

If you find yourself with an under-used ice-cream maker, then you must try making your own fresh cream ice-cream. For best results you'll need one of those machines that has a mini built-in freezer unit that churns as it freezes. If not, a rotating machine that you place in the freezer would just about be acceptable. The addition of crushed meringues is the extra-special touch in this recipe.

Vanilla Ice-cream with Crushed Meringues

**MAKES ABOUT 1 LITRE
(1¾ PINTS)**

2 bourbon vanilla pods (*see* Ingredients note, page 259)

500ml (18fl oz) double cream

150ml (¼ pint) whole milk

175g (6oz) caster sugar

8 egg yolks

2 crushed meringue shells

Using a sharp knife, split the vanilla pods lengthways and scrape out the tiny seeds with the tip of the knife. Scrape the seeds into a saucepan with the cream and milk, then add the pods, too.

Stir in the sugar and bring the milk slowly to the boil, stirring until the sugar is dissolved. Be careful not to let the milk boil over.

Place a bowl on a damp cloth to hold it steady, add the egg yolks and whisk until lightly frothy. Pour the scalded creamy milk on to the yolks in small amounts, whisking well until combined.

Return the mixture to the pan and stir over the lowest possible heat until it begins to coat the back of a wooden spoon and thickens slightly. Do not overheat or it will curdle.

Immediately strain through a fine sieve into a wide bowl and leave to cool, stirring once or twice to prevent a skin forming.

When cold, pour into an ice-cream maker and churn until the mixture becomes a firm slush. Remove and scoop into a bowl. Lightly fold in the crushed meringues and spoon into a freezerproof container.

Freeze the mixture until solid, then cover and store. Use within 2 weeks. Allow to soften for 10 minutes before scooping.

Serving note This ice-cream is mind-blowing with fresh strawberries, blueberries or raspberries, or a mixture of all three.

Variations Use 2 large sprigs fresh rosemary or tarragon instead of the vanilla and serve the rosemary ice-cream with chopped banana, or the tarragon ice-cream with chopped apple.

chocolate & coffee

Chocolate, Vinegar and Oil Cake with Hot Bananas and Lime Juice

This is a great recipe I learned from the famous Chateau Cheval Blanc in the hills of St Emilion. It uses weird stuff such as vegetable oil, water and vinegar, and no eggs. It's the vinegar and soda that cause the cake to rise, but the grandmother of the house told me one golden rule: when the vinegar is added, the cake must be in the oven 30 seconds afterwards. Any longer than this and the mixture will fall when cooking, as it starts to rise even before it reaches the oven.

SERVES 4 (AND MORE)

CAKE

20g (¾oz) butter

375g (13oz) plain flour

85g (3oz) cocoa powder

375g (13oz) caster sugar

2 tsp bicarbonate of soda

300ml (½ pint) water

250ml (9fl oz) vegetable oil

25ml (1fl oz) white wine vinegar

plain yoghurt, to serve

BANANAS

2 bananas

20g (¾oz) butter

juice and grated zest of 1 lime

Butter a 20cm (8in) round cake tin and line it with buttered greaseproof paper.

Preheat the oven to 180°C/350°F/gas mark 4.

Sift the flour and cocoa powder into a bowl and add the caster sugar and bicarbonate of soda. Using a whisk, mix the water in slowly and then the oil. Once these are mixed in, add the vinegar quickly and pour the mixture into the cake tin. It looks rather like a soup – very runny – but don't worry.

Place immediately in the oven for 30 minutes until cooked; it should still be a bit soggy in the middle. Remove from the oven and allow to cool.

Peel the bananas, halve them lengthways, and place them on a small piece of foil. Add a quarter of the butter to each banana, and sprinkle the lime juice and zest over the top. Place under a preheated hot grill and cook for about 5 minutes until golden brown. Remove from the grill.

Arrange each banana half on a plate with a chunk of the chocolate cake and a spoonful of yoghurt.

Chocolate and Ginger Cheesecake

This is possibly the quickest cheesecake in the world. It doesn't need any eggs and requires no cooking. I love entertaining at home, as you might have guessed! This was a quick dessert I devised on the spur of the moment for a three-course dinner when the guests were due any minute. You'll need two items from the sweet section of a deli. The cocoa powder should be the finest you can find – look out for those made by Charbonnel et Walker or the Chocolate Society. To add a spicy flavour, locate a small jar of preserved ginger in syrup – the type you buy in pretty Chinese jars at Christmas time. Serve with soft fruits.

SERVES 4–6

6 digestive biscuits, finely crushed

40g (1½oz) unsalted butter, melted

3 knobs of preserved stem ginger from a jar, plus 3 tbsp of the syrup

3 tbsp good-quality cocoa powder

juice and grated zest of 1 orange

4 tbsp double cream

4 tbsp icing sugar, sifted

300g (10½oz) mascarpone cheese, softened

250g (9oz) fresh strawberries

sprigs of fresh mint, to decorate

Mix the crushed biscuits with the butter and 2 tbsp of the ginger syrup, if using, then press into the base of an 18cm (7in) loose-based flan tin. Place in the freezer for a few minutes to set the crumbs.

Finely chop 2 of the knobs of ginger. Cut the remaining knob into fine strips and set aside.

Blend the cocoa powder with the orange juice, then beat in the orange zest, chopped ginger, cream and sugar. Gradually work the mascarpone into the mixture.

Spread the mixture on top of the biscuit base and place in the refrigerator for about 30 minutes to set.

To serve, push up the base of the flan tin carefully to unmould the cheesecake. Cut the cheesecake into wedges and arrange each wedge on a serving plate. Mix the ginger strips with the remaining ginger syrup (if using). Divide the strawberries between the plates and trickle over the ginger syrup. Decorate each serving with a mint sprig and serve.

The length of this recipe may be a little daunting, but good brioche is like good bread: it needs care, love and attention. The brioche is best made in a food mixer with a bowl, paddle and dough-hook attachment. And the jam needs to be made in advance. I have made a medium chocolate brioche by mixing a plain and a cocoa dough together, but if you are a chocoholic, you could use just a cocoa dough, doubling the amount of cocoa powder. When mixing, simply add the cocoa with the flour, then continue as in the recipe.

Hot Chocolate Brioche with Raspberry and Fig Jam

SERVES 6

675g (1lb 8oz) plain flour

1 scant tsp salt

75g (2¾oz) caster sugar

25g (1oz) fresh yeast

8 eggs, beaten

4 tbsp cocoa powder

250g (9oz) butter, softened, plus an extra 50g (1¾oz) for greasing

TO SERVE

Raspberry and Fig Jam (*see* page 279)

Sift the flour, salt and sugar into the mixer bowl and crumble in the fresh yeast. Using the paddle or beater attachment, mix in the beaten eggs slowly, bit by bit, until a dough is formed.

Mix the dough for a further 5 minutes, then take out of the bowl and divide into two. Put one half back into the machine and add the cocoa powder to it. Continue mixing the chocolate dough in the machine (with the dough hook now) and knead the other half by hand, for a further 2 minutes each. Place the doughs into two bowls, cover with tea-towels and place in a warm put for 20 minutes or until doubled in size.

Place the plain dough into the machine and, on a low setting, slowly add half of the soft butter until it is all combined. Remove this buttery dough from the mixer, and do the same with the chocolate dough and the remaining soft butter.

Butter either an 18cm (7in) brioche mould or a 25cm (10in) loaf tin well and leave to one side. Turn both doughs out on to a cold board and knead together for 2–3 minutes to achieve a marbled effect. Place in the mould or tin and return to a warm place to allow the mix to double again in size: about 20 minutes.

When the dough has risen, preheat the oven to 180°C/350°F/gas mark 4. Brush the dough with the egg yolk and bake in the oven for 45 minutes until golden brown but cooked in the middle. Cool, and serve sliced, fresh or toasted, spread with butter if you like and the cold jam.

Hot Chocolate Fondants

Hands up all those who love a dark and delicious hot chocolate soufflé? Almost everyone, I bet. Well, this recipe is sure to please. If you've ever wondered how chefs manage to bake a pudding with a rich sauce that oozes out, then follow these simple instructions. You can cook the mixture as soon as you've finished making it, but it also freezes brilliantly and can be baked once it has thawed.

SERVES 8

225g (8oz) dark chocolate with at least 60 per cent cocoa solids

4 tbsp double cream

100g (3½oz) butter

35g (1¼oz) ground almonds

2 large eggs, separated

35g (1¼oz) cornflour

85g (3oz) caster sugar

Finely grate 40g (1½oz) of the chocolate and set aside. Gently melt a third of the remaining chocolate with the cream in a small saucepan, stirring well to mix. Remove and leave to cool.

Line a small plate with clingfilm and pour on the mixture. Place in the freezer for about 8 hours until set hard, then stamp out 8 small rounds using a 3cm (1¼in) round cutter. Set aside.

Melt half the butter and brush liberally all over the inside of 8 ramekins. Dust well with the grated chocolate, shaking out any excess. Set the ramekins aside on a baking sheet.

Melt the remaining chocolate (including any shaken-out excess) and butter in a small heatproof bowl over a pan of barely simmering water, or in a microwave-proof bowl in the microwave on Full for 2–3 minutes, stirring once. Do not overheat or the chocolate will 'seize', or turn solid. Scrape this mixture into a bigger bowl, then beat in the ground almonds, egg yolks and cornflour.

Whisk the egg whites in a separate bowl until they form stiff but not dry peaks. Gradually beat in the caster sugar. You may like to use a hand-held electric whisk for this.

Fold the meringue mixture into the melted chocolate mixture. Spoon half the combined mixture into the base of the ramekins, place a chocolate disc on top, then fill each ramekin with the remaining mixture. Smooth the tops of the fondants and chill in the refrigerator while you preheat the oven to 180°C/350°F/gas mark 4.

Bake the fondants in the oven for 10–15 minutes until risen and slightly wobbly, then remove and eat as soon as possible.

Serving note Serve with good-quality ice-cream – coconut-flavoured is especially good.

St Emilion has many good memories for me. My father is a wine judge, one of only two in England for the region of St Emilion, and he used to take me with him when visiting there. I still go every September during the grape harvest. St Emilion is built on a hillside, and has the most beautiful town square with a church in the centre. Among the wine shops are patisseries selling the best macaroons I have ever tasted. The smell of cooking almonds drifts into my dad's house which overlooks the square. And, if I'm honest, that's the real reason I go back – not for the wine. This mousse is based on those macaroons and is seriously, seriously rich.

St Emilion Chocolate and Macaroon Mousse

SERVES 4

280g (10oz) good-quality dark chocolate, broken into pieces

85g (3oz) butter, melted

8 egg yolks and 4 egg whites

115g (4oz) caster sugar

24 small macaroon biscuits

300ml (½ pint) good St Emilion red wine

juice and grated zest of 1 orange

Place the chocolate in a bowl and melt either over a pan of hot water or, better still, in a microwave for 30 seconds. Stir in the melted butter.

In a blender, whisk the egg yolks and sugar together until light and thick (the ribbon stage), then pour into a large bowl.

Clean the blender bowl well and whisk up the egg whites stiffly. Leave to one side.

Take 4 large wine glasses and place 3 of the biscuits in the bottom of each. Pour half the wine into the bottom of the glasses.

Stir the orange zest and juice into the sugar and egg mixture, and then quickly fold in the chocolate, then the egg white, very carefully.

Fill the glasses to halfway with this mousse mixture and then top with the remaining biscuits. Pour the rest of the wine over this and then fill the glasses up to the top with the rest of the mousse.

Place in the fridge for at least a few hours, preferably overnight.

White Chocolate, Whisky and Croissant Butter Pudding

I perfected this dish while working in London. It's ideal for using up slightly stale croissants or, better still, cheap ones from supermarkets near closing time. To be made well, it needs a good-quality white chocolate containing at least 30 per cent cocoa solids, good Scotch whisky and a combination of eggs and egg yolks (see Tip).

SERVES 4

500ml (18fl oz) milk

500ml (18fl oz) double cream

1 vanilla pod

3 eggs and 5 egg yolks

200g (7oz) caster sugar

3 large croissants

25g (1oz) sultanas

25g (1oz) butter, melted

175g (6oz) good-quality white chocolate, grated

3 tbsp whisky

55g (2oz) apricot jam, slightly melted

icing sugar, for dusting

Preheat the oven to 200°C/400°F/gas mark 6.

Pour the milk and cream into a pan, add the vanilla pod, and gradually bring to the boil.

Place the eggs, egg yolks and sugar together in a bowl and mix well.

While the cream is heating, slice the croissants and place in an ovenproof dish, slightly overlapping the pieces. Sprinkle with sultanas and pour over the butter.

Once the cream has boiled, take it off the heat. Add the egg mixture and chocolate and stir well. Set on one side to allow the chocolate to melt, stirring occasionally.

Add the whisky to the cream. Next, using a sieve, strain the cream over the croissants, cover with foil and bake in the oven for 15–20 minutes or until almost set.

Remove from the oven, coat the top with the jam and dust with icing sugar. Caramelize the topping using a very hot grill or, if you have one, a blow torch. This is best served at room temperature, with a spoonful of good ice-cream.

Tip The reason whole eggs are combined with egg yolks is that although the whites make the mixture tough, they're actually needed to make it set. The extra egg yolks make the mixture more smooth and creamy. Please note that overcooking the dish in the oven can cause the custard to curdle.

Honey Mocha Mousse

There seem to be a whole variety of different flavours in this seductively rich chocolate mousse, but believe me, they come together brilliantly. First, make sure you choose a good dark chocolate with at least 60 per cent cocoa solids. To increase the chocolate flavour even further, choose a good-quality cocoa powder, like those from Charbonnel et Walker, the Chocolate Society, or the organic products from Green and Blacks. Also, make sure you use a good honey (*see* recipe introduction for Saffron and honey pears, page 268).

SERVES 4–6

150g (5½oz) dark chocolate

50g (1¾oz) cocoa powder, sifted

1 tbsp clear honey

2 tbsp orange liqueur, eg Grand Marnier or Mandarine

1 tbsp good-quality instant coffee

2 free-range large eggs, separated

25g (1oz) caster sugar

100ml (3½fl oz) double cream

Break up the chocolate and melt either in a heatproof bowl set over a pan of barely simmering water or in a microwave-proof bowl in the microwave on Full for 2–3 minutes, stirring once. Do not overheat or the chocolate will 'seize', or turn solid. Leave to cool slightly, then beat in the cocoa powder and honey.

Gently heat the liqueur in a small saucepan, add the coffee and stir until dissolved. Stir into the chocolate mixture. Leave to cool.

In a large bowl, whisk the egg yolks with the sugar until thick and creamy, and no longer grainy. This is best done with a hand-held electric whisk. With the beaters set on slow, gently whisk in the chocolate mixture.

In a separate bowl, whip the cream until softly stiff. Fold into the egg and chocolate mixture with a large metal spoon.

Place the egg whites in a large grease-free bowl and whisk them until they form soft peaks using clean, grease-free beaters. Fold the egg whites into the mousse mixture using a large metal spoon.

Divide the mousse between 4–6 pretty serving glass dishes or ramekins. Place in the refrigerator to chill for at least 1 hour, but they will keep overnight.

Serving note Serve with fresh raspberries and a ready-made raspberry coulis, or simply a trickle of single cream or runny half-fat crème fraîche.

Safety note This recipe contains raw eggs.

Coffee 'Mushrooms' with Cardamom and Chocolate

This is a good dish for impressing friends, as it makes a restaurant-quality dessert out of bought-in items. It was actually invented while I was at Chewton Glen in Hampshire, working as a pastry chef. Several of the guests undertook a mushroom hunt in the New Forest each year. Their mushrooms were used in a seven-course meal, so we had to create a mushroom-style dessert. This is a much simpler version of that dish. It uses coffee ice-cream 'stalks' with biscuity tuile domes on a sublime cardamom sauce.

SERVES 4

1 x 600ml (1 pint) good-quality coffee ice-cream, slightly softened

250g (9oz) milk chocolate

cocoa powder

icing sugar

TUILES

115g (4oz) butter, softened

140g (5oz) icing sugar

3 egg whites

115g (4oz) plain flour

SAUCE

250ml (9fl oz) double cream

55g (2oz) caster sugar

2 cardamom pods, crushed

4 egg yolks

Preheat the oven to 200°C/400°F/gas mark 6.

To make the 'stalks' of the mushrooms, take four large and four small dariole mounds, and line them with clingfilm. Fill with the softened ice-cream and re-freeze until set hard again.

To make the tuiles, cream the butter and sugar together. Slowly add the egg whites to the mix, and then fold in the flour at the end. Using two large and two small round templates (*see* Tip), spread the mix on to a non-stick baking sheet; you need four of each size. Bake in the preheated oven for 2–3 minutes until lightly coloured around the edges. Remove and place each disc of tuile over an egg cup (or similar) until cold. The soft tuiles will fold over into mushroom cap shapes and become crisp. Lift off carefully and leave to one side.

To make the sauce, combine the cream, sugar and crushed cardamom pods in a pad and bring to the boil. Slowly add to the egg yolks in a bowl, and mix well. Return to the pan and stir over a gentle heat until the sauce has thickened. Pass it though a sieve and leave to cool.

Grate the chocolate bars and scatter the gratings in a circle around the edges of the plates. Spoon the cooled sauce into the middle. Unmould the ice-cream, removing the clingfilm, and stand the 'stalks' upright, one of each size on each plate, in the centre of the pool of sauce.

Turn the tuiles dome side up, dust with the cocoa powder and icing sugar in a small sieve, and place the small mushroom 'caps' on the small mushroom 'stalks', the large domes on the large stalks and the small on small. Serve immediately.

Tip For the templates, through which you spread the tuile mixture to get a perfect circle, you can use margarine tub lids. Cut a circle out of the inner flat piece and then place on the baking tray, lipped side up. Spread the tuile mix over the circular hole with a palette knife, then lift the template off, leaving a perfect circle.

Tiramisu There are numerous versions of this wickedly delicious Italian pud, ranging from the simple to the ridiculous. This is my own variation on the theme, but I warn you it has quite a kick since I use not only rum but also Tia Maria and the coffee liqueur, Kahlua. For best results, try and track down the Italian savoiardi or biscottine biscuits. They hold their texture well even when dipped in the coffee syrup.

SERVES 4–6

1 bourbon vanilla pod
(*see* Ingredients note) or
1 tsp vanilla essence

3 free-range egg yolks

50g (1¾oz) caster sugar

250g (9oz) mascarpone cheese

250ml (9fl oz) double cream, lightly whipped

350ml (12fl oz) strong fresh coffee, cooled

2 tbsp rum

2 tbsp Kahlua

2 tbsp Tia Maria

about 300g (10½oz) savoiardi, biscottine or sponge fingers

2–3 tbsp cocoa powder, sifted

Split the vanilla pod lengthways (if using) and scrape out the seeds with the tip of a knife.

Whisk the egg yolks and sugar with the vanilla seeds or essence until thick and creamy using a hand-held electric or rotary whisk. You can do this in a heatproof bowl set over a pan of gently simmering water for a thicker foam. The mixture is ready when a trail of foam forms as you lift up the beaters.

Remove from the heat (if using) and leave to cool, if necessary, whisking occasionally. Beat in the mascarpone, then fold in the whipped cream. Set aside.

Mix the coffee with the rum and liqueurs. Dunk the Italian biscuits or sponge fingers quickly into the coffee, making sure that they are completely immersed. If using sponge fingers, don't leave in the coffee for more than a second, or they will turn soggy. Arrange the biscuits or fingers in a layer in an attractive glass bowl and top with half the mascarpone and cream mixture.

Repeat with another layer of dunked biscuits or fingers and the remaining mascarpone and cream mixture. Shake the cocoa powder over the top in an even layer, then leave to set in the refrigerator for at least 2 hours.

Ingredients note The best-quality vanilla pods come from Madagascar, and bourbon are the very best. Sold in vials, they are fatter and fuller than the ordinary variety, and better value.

Safety note This recipe contains raw egg yolks.

fruit

Sexy or what! A combination of fruit and herbs sounds weird, but basil and Amaretto, an apricot and almond liqueur, go superbly with each other and with the slightly charred peaches to create an unusual alternative breakfast dish.

Chargrilled Peaches with Amaretto and Basil

SERVES 2

3 firm peaches

1 tbsp olive oil

50ml (2fl oz) water

4 tbsp caster sugar

1 vanilla pod, split lengthways

12 fresh basil leaves

50ml (2fl oz) Amaretto

2 tbsp crème fraîche

Heat a griddle pan on a high heat. Cut the peaches in half and remove the stones. Rub the oil over the cut sides of the flesh. Place the peaches, cut side down, on the griddle pan and cook for about 5–6 minutes without turning over.

Meanwhile, place the water, sugar and split vanilla pod in a pan and bring to the boil. Remove from the heat and allow the syrup to cool and thicken slightly.

Remove the peaches from the griddle and place on two plates, charred side up.

Rip the fresh basil leaves and add to the syrup, then pour over the peaches.

Heat the Amaretto, pour over the peaches and light with a match. When the flames have died down, spoon the crème fraîche into the middle of the peach halves and serve.

I really enjoy mixing and matching unusual combinations of herbs and fruits. The sweet aniseed-like flavour of fresh basil is wonderful with summer berries, and especially complements the flowery fragrance of a ripe mango. The lime syrup offers a refreshing tangy contrast. Consider how the terrine will look as you layer the fruits, and aim for a good contrast of colours. Try a random jumble of colour, like a splatter painting.

Basil-scented Summer Fruit Terrine with Lime Syrup

SERVES 6

6 leaves gelatine

500ml (18fl oz) water

200g (7oz) caster sugar

3 tbsp vodka

1 ripe mango

500g (1lb 2oz) strawberries

250g (9oz) raspberries

250g (9oz) blueberries

about 12 large fresh basil leaves, plus extra to decorate

SYRUP

50g (1¾oz) caster sugar

juice and grated zest of 4 limes

150ml (¼ pint) water

1 tbsp arrowroot

Line a 1kg (2lb 4oz) terrine mould or loaf tin with clingfilm, allowing an ample amount to fall over the sides. Slide the gelatine leaves into a bowl of cold water to soften.

Meanwhile, bring the water to the boil in a saucepan and add the sugar. Stir until the sugar is dissolved. Pour away the water from the softened gelatine and lightly squeeze out any excess water. Slip the wet sheets into the hot sugar syrup and stir for a few seconds until dissolved. Add the vodka, then pour into a jug. Peel the mango and slice into thin strips. Hull the strawberries and set aside any small dainty ones and some perfect raspberries for decorating. Slice the unreserved strawberries.

Half fill a large bowl (a washing-up bowl, for example) with very, very cold water and add as many ice cubes as you can find. Pour a layer, about 5mm (¼in) deep, of the liquid jelly into the base of the terrine mould or loaf tin and place in the bowl of iced water. It should set quickly. Add a layer of fruits of your choice, then pour over a little more liquid jelly. Press down into the jelly any fruits that bob up to the surface. Again, allow to set, then arrange a few basil leaves over the top. Continue adding layers of fruit, jelly and basil leaves in the same way.

When all the fruits are used up and neatly submerged in jelly, place the terrine in the refrigerator to chill completely, preferably overnight. (I place the terrine on a flat plate or tray so that it doesn't accidentally get knocked or disturbed.)

Meanwhile, to make the syrup, place the sugar, lime juice and water in a saucepan and bring to the boil. Mix the arrowroot with 1 tbsp cold water until clear. Whisk into the hot liquid in the pan until it thickens and becomes clear. Pour through a sieve to remove any arrowroot lumps. Stir in the lime zest and leave to cool, stirring occasionally.

To turn out the terrine, hold the tin over a wet oval serving platter or board and shake down firmly. The mould should slip out without the need to dip in hot water. Peel off the clingfilm. Cut the terrine into 2cm (¾in) slices and arrange on serving plates. Drizzle around the lime syrup and serve decorated with reserved strawberries, raspberries, and basil leaves.

Cheat's Ten-Minute Strawberry Gateau

This is one of my favourite desserts when cooking at home with only half an hour to spare. It looks as if you made it specially, but only minutes before you present it in all its glory it was a bought supermarket sponge flan. I used to prepare this at the Hotel du Vin when asked to make cakes for special occasions such as birthdays. One of my chefs would nip out to the local garage shop to buy the flan case or we would use cake or muffins as a variation. Meanwhile I'd whip up the cream and then whiz everything together.

SERVES 4

1 x 250g (9oz) sponge flan case

600ml (1 pint) double cream

25g (1oz) caster sugar

2 tbsp (approx) brandy

750 g (1lb 10oz) strawberries

55g (2oz) icing sugar

115g (4oz) mixed berries (blackcurrants, blueberries, redcurrants)

a few sprigs of fresh mint

SPUN SUGAR TOPPING
175g (6oz) caster sugar

Cut out the centre of the flan, using a 20–25 cm (8–10 in) stainless-steel ring (or the ring of a springform cake tin, without the base). With a sharp knife, carefully cut this disc in half horizontally so you end up with 2 thin discs. Place the ring on a surface or tray, and put one of the discs inside it.

Whip the double cream with the sugar and brandy until thick. Keep in the fridge.

Hull the strawberries. Leave some whole for a garnish (about 10 of the small ones), and cut the rest in half lengthways. Line the ring with the largest strawberry halves, cut side against the ring. You won't need all of them at this stage.

Spoon the whipped cream into the ring and gently press to the edges, keeping the strawberries in place against the sides. Arrange the rest of the halved strawberries over the top. Add the other disc of sponge, pressing it down. Dust generously with icing sugar. Lift the cake on to a plate and remove the ring by carefully warming the edges with a hot cloth and lifting it straight off.

Place the sugar for the spun sugar into a very clean pan and heat. Once it is caramelized – golden brown and sizzling – remove from the heat to cool slightly.

While this is cooling, take a metal skewer and hold it in a gas flame until it is red hot. Use it to score the top of the gateau in lines to create a diamond pattern. Decorate the top with the leftover strawberries and the mixed berries, and decorate with sprigs of fresh mint.

To finish, dip a small spoon into the caramelized sugar and twist it around a steel to create sugar curls. Continue doing this until you have a candyfloss texture. Place this on top of the berries and serve.

Poached Pears with Ice-cream and a Cinnamon and Goats' Milk Sauce

There are no barriers in cooking food, so here I have abandoned tradition and the old-fashioned fruit salad, and gone for a seriously sweet and unhealthy pear dish with lots of ice-cream.

SERVES 2

2 comice pears

200g (7oz) caster sugar

1 vanilla pod

juice and grated zest of 1 lemon

SAUCE

600ml (1 pint) goats' milk

200g (7oz) caster sugar

4 tbsp golden syrup

1 cinnamon stick

1 tsp baking powder

TO SERVE

200g (7oz) good vanilla ice-cream

To make the sauce, place the milk, sugar and golden syrup in a heavy-based pan and bring to the boil. Crumble the cinnamon stick into the milk and add the baking powder. Remove from the heat and stir well as the mix will rise very quickly. Continue to whisk the mixture until it stops rising, then place on the heat again and bring back to the boil, whisking all the time. Turn down the heat and simmer for about 45 minutes, stirring occasionally to prevent the mixture from burning.

Peel the pears, leaving the stalk on, and core them from the wide bottom. Place in a suitable pan with the sugar and vanilla and cover with hot water. Add the lemon juice and zest, and bring to the boil with the lid on. Turn down the heat and simmer for about 20–30 minutes until the pears are cooked, testing them with the point of a sharp knife.

When the sauce is ready, it should be a caramel colour (if it turns dark brown or black and burnt-looking, you weren't stirring enough).

Remove the pears from the pan and drain for a minute on kitchen paper. Place the pears into a bowl, pour the hot sauce over the top and serve with the vanilla ice-cream on the side.

Tip When you add the baking powder to the hot milk and bring it back to the boil, you need to concentrate hard as it could burn very easily. Also the mixture will rise as it comes to the boil. If you whisk vigorously, it will prevent the mixture from overflowing.

Saffron and Honey Pears

This recipe has a wonderful medieval feeling to it and makes a lovely light dessert for the end of a rich dinner. Saffron may be the world's most expensive spice but it is also one of the most aromatic, and a little goes a very long way. Just a couple of pinches of the golden stamens give a good depth of flavour and colour. The best saffron comes from Spain. Stamens with a deep red colour have more flavour than yellow ones – a fact exploited by the cunning spice-producers who wrap the stamens in red transparent paper so that you can't tell the red from the yellow. Check the pack carefully before you buy. Choose a good honey for this recipe, too. My favourite brand, Viadiu, comes from Portugal in a number of different flower flavours.

SERVES 8

2 good pinches of saffron strands

1 lemon

1 orange

300g (10½oz) caster sugar

500ml (18fl oz) water

6 tbsp clear flower honey

8 slightly under-ripe commice pears

Steep the saffron stands in 2 tbsp boiling water for 5 minutes.

Meanwhile, peel the zest from the lemon and orange in thin strips using a swivel vegetable peeler. Squeeze the juice from the lemon. Keep the orange for another use.

Place the zest in a large saucepan with the sugar and water. Bring slowly to the boil, stirring, until the sugar is dissolved. Reduce the heat and simmer gently for about 2–3 minutes. Add the saffron with its soaking water and the honey.

Peel the pears with a swivel vegetable peeler. Using the end of the peeler or the tip of a small sharp knife, remove the core from the base. Leave the stalks in place for decoration. Add the pears to the pan and bring to the boil. Reduce the heat, cover and simmer for about 30 minutes, turning the pears occasionally, until tender. To hold the pears under the syrup, wet a large sheet of greaseproof paper and crumple it, then press it down on the pears. Remove the pears with a slotted spoon and place in a large jar with a tight-fitting lid – Kilner-type jars are the best.

Boil the syrup for 10 minutes to thicken slightly, then pour over the pears. Leave until quite cold before serving.

Serving note I serve these pears with a homemade crème brûlée, but try a mixture of half mascarpone cheese to half whipped double cream flavoured with vanilla caster sugar (*see* Ingredients note, page 274).

Eggy Belffles, Sautéed Tarragon Apples and Fromage Frais

Belffle™ is a name for a type of Belgian waffle, which is available in some supermarkets. They are round in shape with a layer of caramel in the centre. They are a bit firmer in texture than ordinary waffles (which you can use instead, obviously) and hold together well in the egg mixture. You could replace the fromage frais with soured cream or crème fraîche.

SERVES 2

200ml (7fl oz) milk

3 tbsp caster sugar

2 eggs

2 golden delicious apples

2 sprigs fresh tarragon

40g (1½oz) butter

2 Belffles

50ml (2fl oz) fromage frais

Put the milk, 1 tbsp of the sugar and the eggs into a bowl. Using a whisk, mix the eggs in well, then leave to one side.

Cut the apples into quarters and remove the cores. Cut the remaining flesh into 1cm (½in) cubes. Chop the tarragon into fine pieces.

Put 2 pans on the stove and place half the butter in each. Add the apples and the remaining sugar to one, turn up the heat and leave to cook gently.

Meanwhile dip the belffles well into the eggy mix and place into the other pan. Cook for about 2 minutes on each side until nice and brown.

Remove the belffles from the pan and place on two plates with the sautéed apples piled up on top. Add 2 spoonfuls of the fromage frais, and serve hot with the creamy cheese just melting.

Here is a way of dressing up a humble sponge pudding bought from a supermarket. It uses the unusual but heavenly combination of fresh apples and tarragon, with a creamy custard with a hint of cinnamon. I can promise you that, when it is served, no one will ever guess the origin of the sponge.

Steamed Sponge Pudding with Tarragon Apples

SERVES 4

675g (1½lb) ready-made plain treacle sponge pudding

3 golden delicious apples

3 sprigs fresh tarragon

25g (1oz) caster sugar

20g (¾oz) butter

CUSTARD

200ml (7fl oz) milk

200ml (7fl oz) double cream

85g (3oz) caster sugar

1 cinnamon stick, crushed

4 egg yolks

To make the custard, heat the milk, cream and sugar in a pan together with the crushed cinnamon, and bring to the boil. Briefly whisk the egg yolks in a bowl before pouring on the hot milk and cream mixture. Place back on the heat and heat very gently to thicken slightly, but do not boil. Quickly pass through a sieve, and leave to one side.

Heat the pudding as per the instructions on the pack: it's normally best in a microwave.

While the pudding is cooking, core the apples and chop the flesh into small dice, skin and all. Chop the tarragon and sauté with the sugar and apples in the butter. Cook quickly until the apples are golden brown but still firm to the bite.

Tip the sponge pudding out on to a serving plate and scatter the apples around the base. Spoon the hot egg custard around the edge and serve.

Spiced Oranges

This sweet and spicy orange accompaniment is simple to prepare and has the versatility to complement a wide range of sweet and savoury dishes. I highly recommend this served with the creamy Panna Cotta (see page 238).

SERVES 4–6

8 oranges

100ml (3½fl oz) water

100g (3½oz) caster sugar

1 cinnamon stick

3 large pinches of ground allspice

Remove the zest from 4 of the oranges using a swivel vegetable peeler and place in a large saucepan with the water, the sugar and spices. Bring to the boil, then reduce the heat and simmer for 15 minutes.

Meanwhile, cut away the white pith from all 8 fruits. Cut between the membranes to remove the segments, working over a bowl to catch the juice. Add the juice to the pan. Place the orange segments in a heatproof bowl.

Strain the contents of the pan over the orange segments and leave to cool. When the fruit is cool, transfer to the refrigerator to chill.

Brandied Roast Figs

On one of my trips through Italy, I came across a wonderful old grandmother who cooked figs in a wood-burning oven, which she drizzled liberally with butter, sugar and brandy. Just as she was about to draw them from the oven, they caught fire and she simply blew out the flames without turning a hair. Alongside the figs on our plates she plopped spoonfuls of a crunchy, sweet, flavoured cream, with a cocktail of liqueurs and spirits, known as panna montata. This is my interpretation of her traditional recipe.

SERVES 4

200ml (7fl oz) double cream

2 tbsp vanilla-flavoured caster sugar (*see* Ingredients note)

2 tbsp granulated sugar

1 tbsp Cognac

1 tbsp Grand Marnier

1 tbsp kirsch

1 tbsp Brizard (apricot liqueur)

8 ripe figs, as large as you can find

40g (1½oz) butter

4 tsp caster sugar

4 tsp brandy

To make the panna montata, whisk the cream until softly stiff, then fold in the vanilla and granulated sugars, followed by the 4 liqueurs. Scoop into a pretty serving bowl and chill in the refrigerator until required.

Preheat the oven to 220°C/425°F/gas mark 7. Snip off the tops of the fig stalks, then cut the figs into quarters from the top to bottom but leaving the quarters attached at the base. Press your finger down through the centre of each fig to open up like a star. Place in a shallow heatproof dish.

Drop a small knob of the butter in the middle of each fig, then spoon in the caster sugar. Trickle over the brandy and place immediately in the oven. Leave for 6–8 minutes until golden brown with slightly charred tips. If they catch fire as you take them out of the oven, simply give them one big huff and puff and blow out the flames.

Leave to cool for a few minutes, then serve with the chilled panna montata.

Ingredients note You can buy vanilla sugar, but it costs a lot for what is essentially a very simple item. Just stick 2 or 3 vanilla pods in the centre of a bag or jar of sugar and you'll find that the flavour permeates through the sugar. The vanilla pods can be ones that have had their seeds removed for use in a previous dish.

jams, chutneys & dressings

Raspberry and Fig Jam This is good served with the Hot Chocolate

Brioche on page 250. This basic method also applies to the jam recipes on pages 280 and 284.

600g (1lb 5oz) granulated sugar

6 ripe figs, chopped

450g (1lb) raspberries

300ml (½ pint) water

Place the sugar on an oven tray and warm it in a cool oven, at 140°C/275°F/gas mark 1.

Put the figs, skin and all, in a pan with the raspberries and water. Simmer over a low heat until the fruit starts to break up and becomes like a purée.

Add the sugar and a sugar thermometer. Bring to the boil and boil quickly until the temperature reads 104°C/220°F. Alternatively, *see* Tips.

Remove from the heat and cool for about 20 minutes before pouring into clean jam jars. Put the lids on and store in a cool place.

Tips Heating the sugar speeds up the cooking process, as warm sugar dissolves more easily.

If you haven't a sugar thermometer, put 4 small saucers in the freezer compartment of your fridge before you start. When you have boiled the jam for the required time – about 15–20 minutes – pour a teaspoonful on to one of the cold saucers, and leave for a second or two. If a crinkly skin has formed when you push it with your finger, the jam has reached setting point. If not, boil for another 5 minutes and test again.

Plum and Sage Jam

675g (1½lb) caster sugar

900g (2lb) plums, stoned and roughly chopped

200ml (7fl oz) water

10 fresh sage leaves, ripped up

2 pinches of ground cinnamon

Make the jam following the basic method on page 279.

Add the sage and cinnamon when the jam has cooled, stirring them in well.

Peach and Saffron Jam

800g (1¾lb) caster sugar

900g (2lb) peaches, stoned and roughly chopped

1 tbsp powdered pectin

250ml (9fl oz) water

a pinch of saffron strands

Make the jam following the basic method on page 279.

Add the saffron as the jam is cooling. Some fruit lacks the natural pectin that helps jam to set, so powdered has to be added (you'll find it in health-food stores and good supermarkets). Pectin-rich fruits include apples, berries, pears and lemons.

Saffron, which has a unique flavour and a rich yellow colour, must be used with caution otherwise it will mask the flavour of everything else. Saffron strands tend to be better than the powdered version and give a much richer colour.

Chicory and Orange Jam

This is my all-time favourite relish, which I make in batches ready to liven up quick pan-fries. It goes really well with thick king scallops or plump free-range chicken breasts.

MAKES ENOUGH FOR 1 LARGE JAR

1 onion, peeled and chopped

1 fat garlic clove, peeled and chopped

25g (1oz) butter

1 tbsp olive oil

5 heads of fresh chicory, thinly sliced

juice and grated zest of 2 oranges

2 sprigs fresh thyme

75g (2¾oz) caster sugar

250ml (9fl oz) dry white wine

Place the onion, garlic, butter and oil in a large heavy-based saucepan and heat until it starts to sizzle. Gently sauté the ingredients for about 5 minutes until softened.

Add the remaining ingredients and bring to the boil, stirring. Reduce the heat and simmer gently, uncovered, for 30–40 minutes until the chicory becomes transparent and wilted right down.

Meanwhile, preheat the oven to 130°C/250°F/gas mark ½. Place a clean jam jar in the oven to warm. Once the jam is cooked, leave it to cool slightly before spooning into the warmed jam jar. Seal immediately and leave to cool completely. Use within 1 month.

Vodka, Basil and Lemon Jam

900g (2lb) caster sugar

juice of 10 lemons

zest and flesh of 7 lemons
(no pith), chopped

75ml (2½fl oz) vodka

200ml (7fl oz) water

55g (2oz) fresh basil leaves,
ripped

Make the jam following the basic method on page 279.

Add the basil leaves when the jam has cooled.

Strawberry and Black Pepper Jam

800g (1¾lb) caster sugar

900g (2lb) fresh strawberries

juice and grated zest of 2 lemons

200ml (7fl oz) water

2 tbsp cracked black
peppercorns

Make the jam following the basic method on page 279.

Add the black peppercorns while the jam is cooling.

Muscat and Vanilla Syrup

This is a great flavouring syrup that takes very little time to prepare. I store mine in a squeezy bottle – the type you find on the tables of roadside 'caffs'. Actually, you can buy these (new and empty) from catering equipment stores. It is suitable for all sorts of dishes, such as Chicken Breasts with Asparagus and Muscat Risotto (see page 125), or try it trickled over cod and mash. Make sure you buy fresh vanilla pods that are shiny and waxy rather than dried and shrivelled, and ideally the bourbon variety from Madagascar (see Ingredients note, page 259).

MAKES ABOUT 350ML (12FL OZ)

700ml (1¼ pints) muscat wine, or another sweet dessert wine

4 shallots, peeled and chopped

1 fat garlic clove, peeled and roughly chopped

1 vanilla pod, split lengthways (*see* recipe introduction)

2 tsp coriander seeds, roughly crushed

150ml (¼ pint) clear honey

Place all the ingredients in a wide saucepan. Bring to the boil, then reduce the heat and cook on a medium simmer for about 20 minutes until reduced by half. Leave to cool to room temperature, then strain and pour into a bottle. Seal and store, but not in the fridge as it will turn hard. It will keep for several weeks.

Citrus and Vanilla Dressing

This dressing is delicious with shellfish, such as the Lobster, Mango and Rocket Tarts (see page 216), or try it with pan-fried scallops, chicken or salmon. Make sure you use fresh vanilla pods that still have a lovely waxy feel to them. This is a good use for pods whose seeds you have already used. Store the dressing in a screw-top jar in the refrigerator.

MAKES ABOUT 300ML (½ PINT)

juice and grated zest of 1 lemon

juice and grated zest of ½ orange

4 tbsp rice wine vinegar

150ml (¼ pint) olive oil

2 vanilla pods, split lengthways

¼–½ tsp sea salt

freshly ground black pepper, to taste

Place all the ingredients in a screw-top jar – you may have to bend the pods to fit. Screw on the lid and shake to emulsify. Store in the refrigerator until required – it will keep for up to 2 weeks.

Cucumber and Green Pepper Relish

This is similar to a fresh Mexican salsa. It simply involves finely chopping all the ingredients, mixing them together and leaving to marinate for an hour or so. It's best to chop by hand – if you use a food processor you could end up with a sloppy mixture.

SERVES 6–8

½ large cucumber

2 red onions, peeled and finely chopped

2 green peppers, deseeded and finely chopped

6 ripe plum tomatoes, finely chopped

2 fat garlic cloves, peeled and crushed

juice and grated zest of 3 limes

4 tbsp olive oil

2 tbsp chopped fresh coriander

sea salt and freshly ground black pepper

Halve the cucumber lengthways, scoop out the seeds and flesh with a teaspoon. Discard the seeds and finely chop the flesh. Place in a large bowl.

Add the onions, green peppers and tomatoes to the bowl with the crushed garlic, lime juice and zest, oil, coriander, about 1 tsp salt and black pepper to taste.

Mix everything together well, then cover and chill in the refrigerator for 1 hour.

Serving note This fresh relish is ideal for serving with all sorts of grills, roasts and barbecued foods. It's also good as an accompaniment for curries.

Plum Chutney

When I was running the kitchens at the Hotel du Vin in Winchester, after service when everyone else had packed up and gone home, my sous chef Chris and I would often work into the wee small hours, making up new dishes or practising adaptations of old ones. For some reason, that's when our creative spirits ran free. This 15-minute chutney was one of those ideas, which I like to make up in bulk to keep on hand (it keeps for up to two weeks in the fridge). It goes well with pan-fried halibut steaks (see page 64).

MAKES ABOUT 350G (12OZ), OR ENOUGH FOR 1 MEDIUM JAR

500g (1lb 2oz) dark red plums

2 shallots, chopped

1 tbsp olive oil

100ml (3½fl oz) white wine vinegar

3 tbsp water

1 cinnamon stick

100g (3½oz) demerara sugar

Cut the plums in half down the crease, twist the halves in opposite directions and pull apart. Prise out the stones and discard. Roughly chop the flesh.

Place the chopped shallots in a heavy-based saucepan with the oil and heat until sizzling. Sauté gently for 5 minutes until softened.

Add the plums, vinegar, water, cinnamon and sugar. Stir until the sugar is dissolved, then simmer for about 15 minutes, stirring occasionally, until softened and slightly thickened.

Meanwhile, preheat the oven to 130°C/250°F/gas mark ½. Place a clean jam jar in the oven to warm. When the plum chutney is ready, spoon it into the jar. Seal with a lid and leave to cool completely.

drinks

Spiced Bloody Mary
Not really to be drunk before 11am, but good to spice you up and set you on the way for the day ahead. Brilliant for hangover mornings!

SERVES 2

4 tbsp vodka

1 x 200g can plum tomatoes

3 dashes Worcestershire sauce

½ tsp horseradish sauce

3 dashes Tabasco sauce

pinch each of salt, caster sugar and freshly ground black pepper

8 ice cubes

Simply put all the ingredients, apart from the ice, into a blender. Blend until all the ingredients are well mixed.

Divide the ice between two tall glasses, pour the mix over the top and serve.

Black Velvet

SERVES 2

250ml (9fl oz) Guinness

250ml (9fl oz) champagne

A mixture of equal parts of champagne and Guinness, say, 250ml (9fl oz) of each.

Cranberry Juice with Champagne

SERVES 2

250ml (9fl oz) champagne

250ml (9fl oz) fresh cranberry juice

A slightly more refined and fruitier mix than Black Velvet (*see* page 293), but made in just the same way, with equal amounts of champagne and fresh cranberry juice.

Rum and Hot Chocolate
This is a brilliant winter warmer, but it must be made with a good-quality French variety of drinking chocolate, usually available in the special selection aisles of supermarkets. Such varieties are slightly more expensive because they use a higher percentage of cocoa mass.

SERVES 2

French drinking chocolate

dark rum, to taste

Make the drinking chocolate up with hot milk as described on the packet, then pop in some dark rum to taste. You could add some cocoa powder and sugar for a richer drink. And, to make it even more special, leave the chocolate to cool a little then lightly whip some double cream and spoon it on to the top of each cup to resemble a cappuccino.

Menu Combinations

Menus for two

Salad Niçoise, page 183
Parmesan grilled lobster with a lime and chilli mayonnaise and chips, page 101
Cheat's ten-minute strawberry gateau, page 266

Pan-fried mozzarella wrapped in bacon with chutney and sesame seeds, page 182
Roast marinated duck breast with a chicory tarte tatin, page 46
White chocolate, whisky and croissant butter pudding, page 254

Seared scallop and coriander salad with a lime and red pepper dressing, page 103
Rockefeller chicken with lobster and tomato chips, page 42
St Emilion chocolate and macaroon mousse, page 253

Paillard of chicken with mozzarella, prosciutto and sage, page 37
Pineapple and black pepper tarte tatin, page 221

Dinner party menus

A salad of roasted peppers and olives, page 173
Cheat's coq au vin, page 34

Chilli garlic-dressed mushrooms, page 152
Roast pork with balsamic butter bean broth, page 16

Iberico ham with a herby leaf salad, page 186
Sea bass with summer herbs and roasted limes, page 74
New potato salad with truffle cream dressing, page 166

Scallop salad with salted capers and crispy sage, page 180
Loins of lamb with cumin and almond-dressed artichokes, page 10

Bresaola with confit lemon rind and rocket salad, page 171
Pepper-crusted monkfish with mustard dill sauce, page 66

Salad of two smoked fish, page 175
Anchovy and garlic-studded roast lamb, page 12

Brandade of salt cod, page 60
Beef steaks with sun-blushed tomatoes and parsley, page 24

Hot onion bread with garlic and hand-peeled tomatoes, page 201
Pan-fried chicken with chilli beans, fennel and pancetta, page 41
Griddled asparagus with roasted red peppers, page 136
Salmon with wild garlic sauce and champ, page 86

Crispy speck, artichoke and black pudding salad, page 189
Pan-fried cod with vanilla shrimp butter, page 56

Gedi goats' cheese bruschetta with quince and Parma ham, page 206
Warm banana tarte tatin, page 223

Salad of two smoked fish, page 175
Calves' liver with port-flavoured pan juices, page 27

index

Easy Every Day
Previously published as **James Every Day**
by James Martin

First published in paperback in Great Britain in 2012 by Mitchell Beazley,
an imprint of Octopus Publishing Group Ltd,
Endeavour House, 189 Shaftesbury Avenue, London, WC2H 8JY
www.octopusbooks.co.uk

An Hachette UK Company
www.hachette.co.uk

The recipes in this book are taken from the following James Martin titles:
Eating In with James Martin and *Delicious! The Deli Cookbook*.

ISBN: 978 1 84533 667 7

A CIP record for this book is available from the British Library.

Set in Helvetica Neue LT and AGaramond

Printed and bound in China